Fashion after Fifty

A GUIDE
TO REAL
STYLE

Fashion after Fifty

KAAREN ALEXIS HALE

A warm acknowledgement to my collaborator on the first edition, Felice Hodges, artist, collector, and fashion ideal.

First published in 2008
by Kaaren Alexis Hale, in collaboration with Felice Hodges

This revised and updated second edition published in 2024
by Kaaren Alexis Hale, in partnership with
Whitefox Publishing Ltd

© Kaaren Alexis Hale, 2024

ISBN 978-1-916797-21-5
Also available as an eBook
ISBN 978-1-916797-22-2

A CIP catalogue record for this book is available
from the British Library.

Kaaren Alexis Hale asserts the moral right to be identified
as the author of this work.

All rights reserved. No part of this publication may be reproduced, stored in a retrieval system or transmitted in any form or by any means, electronic, mechanical, photocopying, recording or otherwise, without prior written permission of the author.

While every effort has been made to trace the owners of copyright material reproduced herein, the author would like to apologise for any omissions and will be pleased to incorporate missing acknowledgements in any future editions.

Designed and typeset by Typo•glyphix
Cover design by Heike Schüssler
Project management by Whitefox Publishing

Mid-Life Fashion Breakdown

This book is dedicated to all you beautiful women out there who are in the middle of the journey (not to mention your daughters and younger friends) and find the search for the clothes that you need and the look that you crave rather frustrating. You look in the magazines and newspapers and you are either bored or appalled. This book was originally written in 2007–8, but it is still appropriate in its new form and has been extensively revised and updated. We all know about dressing down, but there is a way to do it… Dressing up is a challenge as well, dealing with social and economic issues as we do. So here it is, a guide to having some joy, and a helpful thought or two, as you seek your ideal style.

Contents

Preface — viii

1. How We Got In This Mess. The Short Version — 1
2. So Here We Are. Still Looking For A Look — 15
3. Grabbing Style By The Throat — 25
4. Black Beauty And Colour Me — 29
5. Jeans Are Not Only For Teens — 43
6. Speaking Of Blazers — 49
7. Bohemian Rhapsody — 51
8. The Joys Of Jewellery — 57
9. Vintage — 67
10. Flesh — 71
11. Scents And Sensuality — 99
12. Luxury — 103

13	Sales	113
14	The Cult Of The T-Shirt	117
15	Working Women Of A Certain Age	125
16	The Gravity Of Bathing Suits	131
17	Exercise Gear	139
18	Sunglasses: Age Defiance At The Tip Of Your Nose	149
19	Scarves And How They Work	151
20	Handbags	157
21	Belts And Other Mid-body Experiences	165
22	Our Fascination With Shoes	169
23	The Eternal Feminine	177
24	Who Are You These Days?	179
	Conclusion	192

Preface

The trouble with reaching fifty is that everything starts to change. This is a war of attrition. At sixty, gravity has pulled hard, and the body is not what it was. By seventy there is an urgent need to cover up. Fashion has ignored you but still there is a need to dress. The female ageing process has not been helped by society's worship of youth and airbrushed beauty, and the fashion industry swallowing that whole.

Is it true that old beauty is no beauty, that it is faded and has become invisible? It is true that mature beauty is out of style with fashion designers, and plastic surgeons have made a fortune from this.

'Ageing isn't for sissies,' Bette Davis wisely noted, but we don't need to give up either. Our lack of style mentors and fashion choices is frustrating given the power and wealth of women. So, are we content with what we have? Do we fill our wardrobes with dreary clothes, insensible to the high-spirited girl inside us who craves fashion adventure? No more high heels just because you have hit sixty-five? No way. Get a lower stiletto if your balance is off and carry on.

This book is not about plastic surgery and diets (not that we are morally opposed to them) or looking young again. It is about feeling and looking good despite an ageist fashion industry. It is about nurturing your self-confidence, learning to use fashion to your advantage, finding mentors, and achieving an elegance that is possible for us. Don't forget the Botox.

How We Got In This Mess, The Short Version

Fashion is creativity and self-expression. You can explain your character through fashion, with what you wear and how you wear it. From a very young age, women look in magazines, look at each other, and find an experimental persona. This search and its inspirations changes with regularity. And so, much of fashion is memory, our memories, what we felt when we were very young; the first thrills, the first high heels, the first bra, the first party dress. It is what we continue to feel and experience as we grow older and become more experienced. As fashion distils into our personal style, it then involves what Diana Vreeland called 'Rejection' – rejection of what doesn't suit, what does not explain, what does not enhance. We adjust to fashion and fashion adjusts to us – at least that is how it should be.

My generation was very influenced by the fashions and experiences of our mothers. And they in turn were influenced by enormous, sometimes catastrophic events, e.g. the Depression and global war. Twentieth-century women saw the end of long skirts and the constrictions of corsets. They saw the diminution of the significance of hats. They saw the birth of utility and ease. They saw the slow strangulation of the class system and the opening up of opportunity. There were always fits and starts but the WWI and WWII generation were the pioneers of women's style development.

Growing up in post-war America in the 1950s, women were bosomy, corseted, wore flowing skirts à la the New Look, flashed their ankles, and wore hats and gloves. A proper woman changed her clothes several times a day. There were house dresses for supervising the housework and greeting the postman at the front door: day dresses and tailored suits; tea gowns, cocktail dresses, dinner suits, evening gowns, and dressing gowns. For entertaining at home women wore long skirts and off the shoulder sweaters. Women wore trousers on sporting occasions only, and possibly on a cruise. They wore flared shorts with halters, sundresses, and divided skirts.

European-influenced designers copied the French, and more forward-thinking American designers invented sportswear. Claire McCardell created a relaxed flowing look for women using Native American references like Navajo patterns on wrap-around blouses over long, pleated cotton skirts. She put pleated silk dresses with wide, soft leather belts. Coats were made to match but had a playful softness in their flowing lines. She worked with knitwear and made play clothes. She virtually invented a new American look. This American look took its cue from Europe but with a difference. American women wanted European elegance, but they also wanted ease to go with their newly suburban lives. Suburbs meant cars for everyone. Cars meant travel, movement, independence, and an expansion of the imagination.

Bonnie Cashin used tweed and leather. She made capes and coats, leather bound with string leather ties over matching skirts in multi colours. They were luscious soft tweeds with a definite sophistication. These tweeds were not for country bumpkins.

Anne Klein and Bill Blass made ensembles: elegant coats over matching dresses and tailored skirt suits. Designers like Tina Leser made relaxed evening clothes.

Our mothers wore these clothes, and we admired our mothers. A fourteen-year-old girl wanted to look and dress like her mother. This is a part of our heritage.

Of course, we had our own choices laid out with regularity each season. There were school clothes that consisted of pleated skirts, round-collared shirts, Shetland sweaters and saddle shoes. For parties you wore a taffeta dress with a circle skirt, a scooped neck, a wide belt and baby Louis heels. We collected cashmere sweaters and flat shoes by the dozen. You wore a camel hair or navy wool polo coat or a three-quarter-length car coat. 'Cheap' girls wore angora sweaters, tight skirts and big earrings. That was the look till the end of the 1950s.

When we went off to university the rules changed only slightly. The hip girls played with their wardrobes, they tweaked them with funny old-lady silk collarless blouses, tight sweaters, expensive patterned sweaters, and tailored skirts. We wore tweed suits to college weekends. We wore kilts and tartan skirts and copied the styles from *Mademoiselle* and *Glamour*. Winter was warm coats, mufflers, heavy sweaters, and long woolly socks. Winter was a fur coat handed down from your grandmother. Believe it when we say that vintage is not a new idea. We couldn't wear trousers at first because they were banned from campuses. This was all coexistent with midnight curfews and self-governing women's punishment boards. We were all afraid of breaking rules, being banned, and getting a bad reputation. We were all afraid of getting pregnant. We wore girdles, pointy bras, and wore our hair in ponytails and long bobs. Rebellion from this rigid style came in the form of rolled-up Bermuda shorts, looking hungover, and borrowing clothes from our boyfriends. Cool was a hockey team jacket with varsity lettering. Cool was a sweatshirt with 'Harvard' on it. Cool was a man's shirt with the sleeves rolled up. Cool was what the boys did.

The whole T-shirt industry was yet to be born. T-shirts were Fruit of the Loom or Carter's, were white, loose, had no letters or logos, and rough boys tucked their cigarette packs in the sleeves.

No one worked out, except for crew or football players. No one did aerobics. Gym was an activity you wished to avoid. We chose either golf, folk dancing, or volleyball, remained overweight and miserable about it throughout our college years. We took diet pills to stay up all night and study, and the healthy thing was something your mother told you to do. When we returned home for the school holidays, we wore what our mothers wore. We borrowed their clothes, wore their fur coats to go to the big city, stuffed our feet into stiletto heels and pulled up our hair in beehives. We all wanted to look like Audrey Hepburn in *Breakfast at Tiffany's*, Kim Novak in *Vertigo*, or the original Sandra Dee. We wore little black dresses for dates and there was little youth culture.

All that changed in the mid 1960s. Maybe it was inevitable after the post-war puritanism of the 1950s. With the development of the birth control pill came the miniskirt and the geometric haircut, and then everything changed, seemingly forever. Fashion magazines, which we all read, changed overnight from featuring frosty models in beautiful gowns and jewellery to Twiggy and Jean Shrimpton, dressed by Mary Quant. They were tall and string slender, childish with huge black-rimmed eyes, and they gangled and dangled their long limbs in the shortest and sparest of skirts. We went from being adolescents to women and then little girls all over again, complete with short skirts, Mary Jane shoes, and tiny little tops, dresses our mothers would have loved on us at nine, and that were now associated with the Youthquake, a new world made up of people under thirty.

It has probably taken all of us years to understand that this attitude in fashion that eliminated adulthood oddly coincided with the Women's Movement. The designers have simply followed this contradictory trend. On the one hand, women were liberated from the constrictions of the past. On the other hand, the fashion industry no longer designed for women but for girls.

In the 1970s we saw the Japanese come and deconstruct our ideas about clothes. We were encouraged to wear trousers with three-quarter legs, sweaters with holes, dresses with shredded seams, everything in non-colours. This developed into complex origami shapes that didn't conform to the body, and by conforming to this new anti-fashion, we were ultimately the most fashionable. We wore strange black hats and heavy, flat boots. Dr. Martens shoe styles, masculine and aggressive, became a cult look. Simultaneously a few women designers made complementary styles emphasising ease of dress. Sonia Rykiel perfected sweater dressing with chopped-off jersey trousers and tiny fitted shoulder-padded sweaters that featured stripes and bows. These you wore with boots and funny little flat broad-brimmed black felt hats. Jean Muir developed a fabulous jersey fabric that clung but did not reveal and suited women, especially dancers.

The financial climate changed in the early 1980s from economic stagnation and high interest rates to a burgeoning, no holds barred stock market, and suddenly style went off in a new direction. Skirts, along with the market, climbed shorter and shorter, and Karl Lagerfeld at the reinvigorated Chanel was king. His goddess was Ines de La Fressange. For a fleeting time the magazines featured a beautiful model woman, someone with the sophisticated features to add to and stylise a look that was glamorous, playful, tough minded, and luxurious. Chanel had always designed elegant useable clothing that featured accessories and a woman's own attitude. Women wore Chanel, and still do as a combination statement of taste, femininity, and status. But this lady-like, sophisticated look segued in the late 1980s into non-existent skirts and shoulders like Samurai warriors.

Lagerfeld led the way with his aggressively accessorised style, à la *Dynasty*, but St Laurent as a guru was his equal. He, having made his reputation in the late 1950s and early 1960s, became the intelligent choice for many fashionable women. He developed a modern look which was a carefully thought-out play on gender and role. Trouser suits, loose shift dresses, blazers with brass buttons, exotic harem pants, bellhop jackets, leather jackets and skirts, 'transparent fabrics', tuxedo jackets and matching trousers for evening called 'le smoking', high heels with trousers, bitter, contrasting colour combinations – acid green with burnt almond. He worked out these themes every season, adjusting lengths and shapes. We all looked forward to his Rive Gauche collection because it meant instant resolution of the age-old problem of 'what to wear'. You bought a pair of flannel trousers, a gabardine skirt, and a perky, curvy coloured jacket to go with them both. You bought a draped dress to wear to a cocktail party or dinner, a fur-trimmed raincoat for day and a black dress or suit for any occasion that warranted dressing up. He had a variety of sweater styles in unusual colours which you mixed and matched to create your look. To finish off he had chunky costume jewellery, stylish shoes, fabulous studded belts, and a few hats.

We never worried about looking right. No matter how old you were at the time there was an excitement and a modernity, a cleanness of line, a kind of liberation that came from a disciplined style that made you feel correct. You never felt defensive or apologetic about yourself. St Laurent was expensive and grown-up but at the same time a bit rebellious. We would wait for the sales if we couldn't do the beginning of the season. He was enormously influential on the High Street. There was something for a young woman, with hopes and dreams of being stylish, and for her mother. And if he were designing today, we would all be happier.

There were other favourites, of course, especially the ultra-feminine Emanuel Ungaro. Ungaro's clothes were what the French called 'flou'. They had softness and movement, colour and pattern, they were tucked and ruched and flirty. Even if he did black leather, it was gathered and moulded to ease itself onto the body. His man-tailored trouser suits were feminine and cut close to the body. There was nothing to compare to the sexy Ungaro cocktail dress in jersey or silk crepe.

But alas the zeitgeist changed as the social and economic landscape mutated, bringing confusion. The financial distress of the 1990s brought in social resistance, Grunge, and minimalism. Grunge was a reaction to the padded shoulders and social demarcations of the 1980s excesses, brashness, elitism, and collapsed dreams. Grunge was a social reaction to success, mobility, and snobbery. It was the rejection of excess. Minimalism too, the rejection of colour and pattern, creative design ideas, was an expression of disgust with the power dressing of the 1980s.

There have always been these actions and reactions in fashion, historically, but soon we women were dealing with entirely different phenomena. The first phenomenon was the amalgamation and incorporation of the fashion industry. Maybe Bernard Arnault, CEO of LVMH, is the saviour of fashion houses and designers and maybe not, as time has begun to tell. He is one of the richest men on the planet and the so-called fashion industry, especially for us, is in chaos. The industry always laboured with boom-and-bust financing and a manufacturer with one or two bad seasons could easily go out of business. There was and is always panic in this business of ideas, ephemera, ego, and rapidity of change. Louis Vuitton/Moët Hennessy (LVMH), as a fashion conglomerate, attempted to lessen the financial risks to one designer's business by spreading it amongst others who were more successful in a particular season. Trouble is, eventually everyone is measured by the same quarterly results criteria. In a public company there is little tolerance for unprofitable divisions. So what happens is homogenisation, stifled creativity, and more and more emphasis placed on those things that sell well: accessories, bags, shoes, and perfume. There isn't a great deal of time for a new designer to develop a signature, to evolve, to experiment in a subtle and incremental way, and an established designer gets caught in the trap of predictability.

There is an emphasis on sensation, eccentricity, change for change's sake to capture the imagination of the powerful fashion press, and two contradictory trends have emerged, both based on the great common denominator of SEX. On the one hand the designer has less to say. He or she must follow the trend. The bandwagon and climbing on board or clinging to its sides is common business intelligence. Thus advertising and sensationalised promotion is much more important. And sex sells everything, as Joni Mitchell puts it in a song. Grunge has mutated into combat trousers and tattoos, the tightest and most revealing of tiny tops and bottoms, the highest sandals, the wildest hair, vulgarity. Minimalism is the last refuge of the bored and frightened. There is a limit to the number of heavyweight cashmere sweaters, terribly tasteful shift dresses, and sleeveless coats even a minimalist can buy.

Fashion minimalism was always about clean lines and clear colour. It was about form following function. It was, originally in the days of Claire McCardell and Bonnie Cashin, about modern, comfortable, corsetless clothes, not featureless clothes that flatter and describe no one. And whoever said black was the only minimalism? Minimalism is one diamond stone in a solitaire. Minimalism is a pair of perfect skin-coloured gloves. It all got lost in the stampede to assure profits in an insecure business full of insecure people and mammoth egos. And as the advertising and promotional budgets loom, ever more enormous and extreme, the smaller designer is either pushed to the wall, withers on the vine, or, worse, is bought out to become part of the 'wall of sound' that is high fashion today.

Under Tom Ford, Gucci became a destination brand, a place to go to acquire cachet. In its progression, the promotional aspects, the perfume, the advertising, became more and more daring, while the actual product line – the clothes, bags, belts, coats, and sweaters – remained essentially what they had been from the first collection: lots of black, crotch tight, bottom hugging, vulgar, and relatively expensive. The brand had also become a combination lifestyle label and cliché.

The takeover of uber-French YSL by Gucci, an Italian company headed by an American designer, was the height of a kind of hubristic presumptuousness. No one we know, with a few notable exceptions, ever walks into the shop. Why? The wrong message. An uncomfortable shopping experience in a dark and unwelcoming place, and the feeling that 'There is no there there', as Gertrude Stein once said about her hometown in Oakland, California. Like so many fashion houses it became a brand based on hype and the endless tasteless recycling of St Laurent's adoration for women. However, in today's market it still presents a choice of re-examinations of the originals, but the thrill for me is gone. As with most current brands, it has branched into handbags, in my view derivative, and shoes, which feature the homage platform, which is well loved by those of us who are under six feet tall. They add authority and glamour with anything: jeans, long and short dresses, cropped trousers!

Along with the sex sells everything approach go Versace and Dolce & Gabbana. In their sales approach they are similar. In their underlying philosophy they are somewhat different. And it is instructive to analyse the differences because it is possible still to locate some style within these brands.

First, Versace. Versace became the avatar for complicated expensive flashy sleaze somewhere in the 1990s. His fantastic homes, his propensity for chain mail, peekaboo, and bare flesh, dutifully noted by the press, made him the fashion equivalent of *Hustler's* Larry Flynt. Models clamoured to wear his revealing bright, tight, short frocks. Even though the dresses were not really shocking, what was challenging was the advertising attitude behind them, that his buying public needed an image of sexual aggressiveness. After his murder, apparently by a disgruntled stalker, his sister Donatella took over the brand and enlisted the aid of models and actresses to assist in its continued promotion as sexy dressing. But if you were to walk into Versace today you would probably find that it is basically selling frocks and pastel suits. It's a question of getting past the hype, the door, and the ice-cool sales staff.

If Versace's image is sincerely tasteless and a paean to zips, studs, holes, and see throughs, then Dolce & Gabbana is the humorous take on the same subject. D&G believe in underwear. Every garment has an underslip or brassiere that is supposed to support, build confidence or bosoms, or both. Dresses have endless laces and grommets, things are shirred like Austrian blinds, and tight to the body. Everything has either a leopardskin lining or detail in this world of Sicilian movies via the 1950s. If there were a style that said Gina Lollobrigida, this is it. And yet, if you bring yourself to look more closely you will find razor-tailored coats, wearable sweaters, flowered garden party dresses, and some funny witty jackets with fake fur trim. Trouble is there are just too many bondage closures on everything. Fashion addicts are prepared to give up comfort for a look, but it isn't for everyone.

Which brings us to the quintessential designers of our time. John Galliano fell into the category of More is More. Like so many creative people, he started off with an inventive, witty, somewhat historical view of fashion design with a flair for cutting and shape. Under the protection of a large conglomerate he has become a kind of ringmaster of the outrageous, the Marcel Duchamp of the frock. He was an enormous influence in terms of what drives the fashion industry, i.e., the selling of more bags and accessories. But the commercialism exceeded the creativity. His personality apparently could not keep up with the business demands. Sadly, in a chaotic moment, induced by medical intervention and alcohol, he lost it all at a bar, was reported for extreme bigotry and disappeared from the cutting edge of the fashion biz. He is probably lurking somewhere as a consultant or perhaps he has retired to a retreat in the Mediterranean. He had his day. His efforts were a paean to creative genius if not madness. A sad ending to a great showman.

There is one designer, Miuccia Prada, who has consistently gone against the sex with everything trend but whose take on style is ironic, postmodern, and has an almost mystical attraction. Could it be her education and devotion to Marxist theory?

She started her fashion progression from her grandfather's luggage and handbag business for the carriage trade in Milan, with near revolutionary practical black nylon handbags for women with careers. She then marched along with quirky reworkings of housedresses of the 1950s, perhaps a political statement about the lives of women. Now she has worked through, in an eccentric way, most of the trends of the last century. If there was an unfortunate cut or style of the last fifty years, Miuccia has taken it, given it a good kick up the rear, and transformed it into something strangely desirable. If women are worried about wrinkles in their clothes, she designs skirts which are about wrinkles. If uneven seams are a bugbear, whole dresses are envisioned with asymmetrically conceived seams up the sides. If you are small and neatly made with no proportional inconsistencies, you just might get into one of her suits. They are cut close to the body in a somewhat unforgiving way and so not everyone can find their size. She designs coats that remind you of your grandmother or your school days but are oddly provoking. She has a nice little line of sweaters that cling.

She makes transparent wispy little blouses which can transform a conservative suit. She has shoes which are unparalleled in their discomfort but have strange iconic chic. In other words, in the face of the youth cult, and against all odds, and despite her primary market – the young, the slight, the skinny, the petite – she produces something interesting season after season. She has an eclecticism in her work. It's as if she was called in by the Master of all Fashion to correct other people's work with her own unmistakable signature. It is always inspiring to go to her shops and look at the racks. The clothes have a personality which seem to transform the wearer into someone edgier and cooler. On a separate note, I would myself discourage the brand's concentration on sneakers or trainers as they are called in London. They are becoming a bore. But needs must for profits, I suppose. It will fade like most things.

It is important to mention Ralph Lauren. He has been a driven entrepreneurial prince whose lifestyle vision is epitomised by the sumptuousness of his stores. Here the consumer can find unchallenging clothes and accessories in a comfortable seductive setting. The mise en scenes have changed over the years from English country house to Manhattan penthouse, but he started out selling a sharp menswear look to women which was sexy, well-tailored, and young. He segued into the American West, Native Americans, pioneers, country squires, and Hollywood stars of the 1930s. His styles suit every setting, and if you are going on holiday, wherever north, south, east, or west, he can supply a costume for the occasion in his vast dry goods stores. Superb advertising offers conservative tweeds and velvets that are slightly adjusted for trend every year. One season, there are ruched trousers that only people with serious vitamin deficiencies would even attempt, other years dresses and blouses that take you from town to country efficiently. There is the seriously expensive Miss Marple look and the near-naked very demanding evening gown collection. His design team is hooked on vintage-style fabric. These clothes are safe choices, never ridiculous, never exactly fashion. His profits derive from multi-coloured shirts with logos and men's clothes. He is a genius merchandiser with a taste and imagination coloured by endless hours in the cinema. Sports clothes come cheaper at Lululemon and Nike, but let's give him five stars for ambience, glamour, and service, and at least two forks for clothes.

And then there is Mr Giorgio Armani. Armani is ease. Armani is comfort. Armani is throwing away formality. Armani is gender playfulness. Armani today is a recognisable look, an attitude, at best utility, and at worst conformity. He still makes fashion that murmurs and doesn't shout. He has drifted a bit away from his roots, which were to dress Milanese women with money and jewellery and tans, but he has had a powerful idea that continues to work for a lot of women, the idea that clothes are a uniform, much like menswear. It enables you to travel, to work, to perform, to care, to be respected, to be taken seriously. It is therapeutic, like herbal tea. It does not excite, stimulate, or offend. It reassures and it is a good choice when you are feeling fragile. You can be perfect or deeply flawed. His look has enough of a message to transcend physical imperfection. It imposes a personal vision on the woman who wears it and perhaps in a funny way makes her freer to be her real self. It is protective. Recent purchases prove that there is a style out there that is smart, elegant, easy to wear, and comforting. In clothing ourselves we need to be comfortable, which brings me to the current trends.

Current trends are mixed. There is an emphasis on sport references, soft fabrics, loose cuts, but as I might quote Paul Smith, there is a loss of focus, cut, fit, and quality. This was mentioned by the style editor in the *FT*. I concur. Tailoring is vital to any woman whose body is not perfect. And tell me whose is? Tailoring creates a shape, a definition and with it a sense of confidence. Until the industry finds it possible to retrace their steps and forget the so-called EASY, and focus on making money, things won't change that much. The demand must be made for BETTER.

So Here We Are, Still Looking For A Look

They say that sixty is the new fifty. Well maybe seventy is the new forty! Who knows, it depends on the individual and how many drugs she is taking! We are well preserved, toned, dieted, dyed, and lifted. We have careers, we have done the corporate things, we are into charitable giving and introspection about the state of the planet. We have our icons and have seen them come and go and we are still desperately seeking clothes. Trouble is these days we cannot find either the clothes or the image that we need to project our own hard-won sense of self-esteem and sensuality.

The most common complaint you hear from a middle-aged woman is that none of the designers are making clothes for them. Where is the chic, easy, sexy look that we grew up with? Today's designers make clothes for girls of sixteen and try to sell them to women of fifty-plus. And so there are thousands of handbag choices and shoes out there and nothing to wear them with. Women with good bodies, attitude, plenty of savvy and potential style, are being left in a kind of shoppers no-woman's land. They either sign up for the mature headmistress or barmaid look or resign themselves to what is in the deep recesses of their wardrobes. Sadly, a retiring designer friend of mine says that FASHION is dead and that now anything goes, so you have to thread your own way through the maze.

Many older women lose their way very early. Society's values don't expect a woman to stay feminine and sensual. They were not taught from birth the regimes of care. They are overloaded by cultural norms of Barbie dolls and cartoon characters. Why aren't we being catered to? There are millions of us with money in our purses. We are richer and have more insurance, as the heroine of *Fried Green Tomatoes* said, and yet there is no style or personality template on which our imagination can light: television personalities with their plastic faces and pastel pant suits? Movie stars and models who wear the minimum? Check out Rihanna. Not that I don't admire her nerve, but REALLY? We see politicians whose clothes sense is based on causing the least offence to the greatest number. And the fashion crowd who express themselves in the media but are always in black and the latest handbag? Lately we have to contend with so-called fashion idols who wear gigantic fake animals on their shoulders for fun. Not possible.

Vogue, which was once the bible of taste and innovation, is, in my view, now the moral equivalent of the old *Forum* magazine, a sex clinic, an ideological document, and a constant source of memory retrievals by people with terrible lives. The clothes go from grunge to gorilla. The models are beautiful and very young, mutable, and extraordinary but they are impossible to relate to. Their endless legs, their look of sexual availability, their flawless faces helped by the airbrush, their muteness. They are not real. We used to gape in a kind of adoring recognition at the likes of Jean Patchett or Suzy Kendall, Jean Shrimpton or Lauren

Hutton. They looked human and we could relate to them. We yearned to be like them. We idolised them and the clothes they wore.

They seemed of this planet, better of course, but somehow in the same world. We need mentors and we need clothes. Because they renew our ideas about ourselves and reconfirm our egos. Because fashion is a refresher course in feminine attraction. It evolves and so must we. What we don't need are images of models who are not in the least like us. What about a Jane Fonda lookalike?

This is a fashion guide for the grown-up woman, who has been there, done that, shopped until she has dropped, arrived home in confusion and desperation and cried out in sartorial pain for help. She screams, 'I have nothing to wear!'

If we cannot choose from the things that are out there, then we must create awareness in the fashion world to hear our cries. And while we are waiting, we can learn and understand how to find what we need and can use to create this better self, over and over again.

Where do we start to lighten and brighten up? First, we start with the condition of our bodies, our health, and our attitude. At this time of life, there is ever more need to maintain – in fact, high maintenance is not an option, it's a necessity. We need to sleep well, eat sensibly, take vitamins, have massages, monitor our hair colour, have a facial now and again to freshen our skin, and we must give ourselves time. High maintenance starts with the body, and moves on to the spirit, the imagination.

Ask yourself, what and/or who do I want to look like? Each one of us has a heroine of style in our minds. There are so many icons in the twentieth century: Audrey and Katherine Hepburn, Jackie Kennedy, Marilyn Monroe and Julie Christie, Diane Keaton and Barbra Streisand, Jane Fonda and Mrs Thatcher.

We are all of these icons; we have absorbed them into our lives and memories and there are little bits of their influence that come out when we think about ourselves and when we go shopping. Kate Hepburn is androgenous, boyish but reeking of spirit and personality. Audrey Hepburn is stylish, vulnerable, tough-minded underneath, feminine and loving. I love them best, but I have a soft spot for Mrs Thatcher, who made it in a tough male-dominated world, keeping her femininity. It is interesting to read that Golda Meir, one of the twentieth century's icons, dressed like a cleaning woman and yet had dozens of male devotees for love and politics. You never can tell. Your personality is paramount!

One of the looks out there is so called Casual Comfort. Let us define what that is. How does that translate into stylish (and not 'I don't care' or worse?) Should it be seen as a statement of our self-confidence and refusal to be trussed up like chickens or made to feel insecure? It is a trend that many of us wish to follow, but not without some reservations of taste and age. Is it a passing phase, or is it, and should it be, a part of our lives and a way of expressing ourselves?

We have been in miniskirts, Japanese oddities, stretchy dresses à la Alaïa that needed no underclothes. Jeans of all sizes and shapes pack our cupboards: ones for walking, ones for cleaning out the garage, some for fashion with a fancy jacket, some dark, some light. We have done it all as we have grown up, and now we are confronted with Casual Comfort. Are we ready for pyjamas in the street?

This is the latest wheeze in a long line of absurd but tempting looks. If, for example, you were off to the beach and had a strong sun allergy, this look is for you. In fact there is a wonderful Agatha Christie mystery (*Evil Under the Sun*) featuring David Suchet as Hercule Poirot, where the murderess runs down to the beach to assist in the killing of her rival in a fabulous floaty pyjama outfit with a charming large straw hat. This could work with open-toed sandals with wedge heels, with no intentions of wickedness.

You find yourself in Antibes, or Palm Beach, or Nantucket, and you are out for lunch. Drawstring lightweight silk or linen trousers with an open jacket over your bathing suit, and a large sheltering hat to keep the sun off your freshly done hair. Large sunglasses and plastic chains complete the look. Carry a straw handbag with a tied-on linen scarf. Wear your pyjamas on the Amalfi coast or Capri. Wear them at the beach club. Not for the city. Versions of this can be found in one form or another at Valentina Kova, the Palm Beach emporium that specialises in elegant, comfortable creations for day and night. I love her trousers and loose silk shirts, not to mention silky jackets and dresses that emphasise ease and the personality of the wearer.

--- --- --- --- ---

Lycra? A curse or a blessing? You are off to the gym. Unless you have the body of an eighteen-year-old supermodel, do not attempt flesh-coloured bicycle shorts with a midriff-revealing bra top. Rather, if you are out for a brisk walk down to the shopping street, you could wear stretchy leggings with a loose-cut linen dress or a poncho. Leggings can suit the middle-aged and older as long as there is a bit of masking of the less than perfect parts. Take a good look at your rear view in your mirror before you leave home! I suggest white leggings instead of black. It is counter-intuitive of course. They don't make you look heavier. They simply make you look lighter in feeling and mood and go with all kinds of longish tunic tops. Stay off the logo T-shirts.

--- --- --- --- ---

Try this look. A long skirt, full, pleated, or a buttoned kilt, white, black, navy, or a small pattern. Clunky sandals on a platform. A white T-shirt, or a matching or complementary cotton, silk, or linen sweater. Do not tuck in. Push up sleeves. If you have sun spots on your legs dab a bit of face foundation on them with a make-up brush. No tights, please. Wear a straw hat fedora-style. No baseball caps. They are for the young only unless you are playing pickle ball. Long dangling earrings, real or fake. Baroque pearls. Dinner-plate-sized clip-on earrings.

Carry a woven bag over your shoulder (could be Bottega leather or, even better, fabric as weighs less). Never leave your bracelets at home. Try plastic, Bakelite, silver, gold, straw, bangles. Leave your fabulous jewellery in the safe.

If the weather looks iffy, a leather jacket will be cool.

— — — — — — —

Try this jeans look for stylish summer dressing down. White or off-white full-legged jeans with fringed bottoms. Fitted white shirt, cotton or linen worn outside the trousers. Tie a colourful sweater around your waist and hips. This look is practical as well as chic because the weather might change! Wear medium-high espadrilles with everything. They lend height and stability, as you are balancing on wedges, and a chic casual look. There is no need to buy canvas shoes at Chanel for a fortune when you can find far less expensive canvas espadrilles that bring up images of Brigitte Bardot in St Tropez. Ankle straps add balance! Go to Capri just to buy them!

— — — — — — —

I know you love your sneakers (trainers) but unless you are running a marathon, taking the dog for a brisk walk, or cleaning out the garage, wear shoes that emphasise your ankles, your well-turned legs, your shapely knees, your polished toenails. These are part of your feminine allure. Ankle boots on a low heel do the same thing for winter casual dressing.

There is a smart look for everyone (all seasons), and I adore it. Long coats. Summer: silk, linen, cotton drill. Winter: wool, cashmere. If you are slim, a black A-line coat is a wonderful look worn over jeans, cropped trousers, wide-legged trousers, long skirts and a sweater. If you are shorter, a knee-length shape is flattering and youthful, over jeans, cropped trousers and ankle boots, chunky heeled shoes. Spring/summer wear pale, blonde, camel colours over white flannels, cream or white full-legged jeans, linen trousers, with polo shirts. Trench coats are good if you are small-waisted. Remember not to tie the waist too tight. It is cooler and more chic to wear them looser. It is only allowed if you still have a tiny waist like Scarlett O'Hara. To avoid the look of channelling Raymond Chandler's detective Sam Spade, try your trench coat over a black leather skirt and black turtleneck with low-heeled court shoes. Add a fedora for fun. You will look more Lauren Bacall than Bogart. Wear hair loose, well cut, with dangling diamond earrings, either real or Georgian paste!

One favourite look: a long unlined silk coat with a streamer. This incredible bathrobe style can pair with anything from summer jeans to long skirts, linen trousers, narrow- or wide-legged, paired with white or black T-shirts, high-heeled espadrilles, the most ultra-glamorous at Valentino, making for an unforgettable plus comfortable look.

Practise your walk! Glide, do not lurch. At a certain age we can no longer cope with very high-heeled shoes. But we can improvise with a heel height that allows us to gain inches and a feeling of youthfulness. Another bugbear are flats. They do nothing for anyone under 5 ft 10 inches. I love the gladiator-look sandals, replete with straps, under a long colourful silk coat with capri trousers, bright white T-shirt, and a stylish necklace or earrings.

— — — — — — —

Alas miniskirts are not for us. We once wore them with brio. Thigh-high boots. Tight sweaters. Geometric haircuts, black or red fingernails. We CANNOT GO THERE AGAIN. Instead, a casual haircut by an expert who understands who and what you are today. Make sure your hair is in good condition and doesn't look like a helmet or a furry doormat. Try long swishy gypsy-styled skirts in taffeta, lace, silk charmeuse, cotton or polyester. These are so adaptable. Wear with a silky sweater or a John Smedley cotton and merino wool cropped, loose hip-length T-shirt, or a silk blouse tucked in or out with a thin belt. If you are long-waisted a wide belt gives a sporty look, worn at the waist or just below. This look goes from lunch to dinner and after.

Wide-legged silky trousers can do the same thing. You look dressed, but comfortable. Because you are comfortable you have a happy relaxed look on your face. That alone equals YOUTHFULNESS.

— — — — — — —

Shirt dresses are always in style. All you must know about them is yourself. These are good in block colours with all kinds of sandals and shoes. Just please leave the trainers for exercise and hiking. Each accessory you don makes a different mood. The shirt dress can be undressed by leaving off the belt and wearing loose, especially in warm weather, or made smarter with a good-looking belt or a pretty folded scarf around the waist. You can add a chain belt or a waistcoat or a tiny, short cardigan. Accessorise with a hat, wide and romantic or a mannish fedora. Hair back behind the ears or tied up, long earrings. Carry a woven bag or tiny clutch for keys and lipstick.

Think colour. Think pink. I am not recommending Little Bo Peep. I am thinking strawberries and cream, fuchsia, raspberry, shocking and purply pink. I am thinking chartreuse, a fabulous colour for literally every complexion. For a casual and sporty look, great pink sweats with matching sweater, pale lace-ups, and a big colourful shawl.

Speaking of shawls: you can never have too many. Collect them wherever you go. Silk, cashmere, blend, fine cotton gauze, knitted and ethnic patterned. This is the easiest accessory of all. Think ottoman-shaped trousers, a white cotton or silk shirt, a low-slung belt, low-heeled shoes, and a fabulous scarf. This is casual/comfortable, and chic, and WORKS ANYWHERE.

Rule of thumb: avoid trying to dress like your daughter or granddaughter. Compete with your peers – and why not, we are only human. Take something off before you leave home (preferably a piece of jewellery and not your trousers!) and for safety's sake look where you are going. The doctors say that the worse thing to do at this point in time is to FALL.

Grabbing Style By The Throat

Let's start with people we admire, i.e. the Latin woman, Italian, French, South American. They appear to have great innate self-confidence. They seem to deal with the limits of age better than their English and American sisters. Their societies, though more tradition bound, don't seem to discard the older woman, deny her opportunities for pleasure, dismiss her as a physical anomaly. There are any number of Italian and French women of a certain age who are as attractively turned out as they ever were without being overdressed, over made-up, over lifted, or ignored. They develop their fashion personalities over time. Nina Ricci once said, 'Know yourself before you get dressed.' They are taught style at an early age by their mothers. There is no guilt in a French or Italian woman's attitude about making herself look good. And there is no obvious sense of panic about the natural passage of time. Oh yes, there is a little nostalgia for past glories, but they get on with it and develop what they have. They look at their strong points, they care for themselves, as a ritual. They value being a woman. They value experience, knowledge, sophistication, and their sexuality. They have been taught to be proud of their femininity and that's why they look good. We must learn the same skills. Constructive self-criticism, not self-hatred. Learning to judge yourself objectively within your own peer group not by comparing yourself to a twenty- or thirty-year-old woman.

Not to get too pretentious, but Dr Jung, the great psychoanalyst of dreams, once said, 'We cannot live the afternoon of life according to the program of life's morning; for what was great in the morning will be little at evening, and what in the morning was true will at evening have become a lie.' We need to focus on the evolution of personal style.

―――――――

But before you can get to the details of searching for and building a wearable and affirmative wardrobe, let's deal with the BIG CLEANOUT.

Clear the decks and create space. This is a good idea because it examines and reveals the extent of your self-delusion. The process will pinpoint the necessity to think anew. Let's call this THE DECADE DUMP.

But how to clear out the emotional wreckage of years of worn, no longer fashionable, inappropriate and useless items in the wardrobe? There is a philosophy that must be absorbed first.

We are older. We have lived. Some of the favourites you treasure and horde no longer suit the person you are. Would you wear at twenty what you thought was fabulous at fourteen? Women age in decades. So go into the wardrobe and observe closely the following advice.

Do you wear it regularly? Is it something for a special event? Do you love it and every time you wear it you feel good? Do you take it out, put it on and immediately discard it? Do you have a group of favourites? Does your partner, if you have one, look at you quizzically when you parade yourself before them in this item? Do they say sweetly, 'Is that what you are wearing tonight?' If they do, consider giving it to a worthy charity or decide very seriously if you will ever wear it, even out of their sight? Do you feel dull and listless in this style? Do you feel bloated? The last time you walked into a room in it, did you wish you had worn something else? Can it be used in a number of ways, made to work for travel, country, casual, dressed up? In other words, is it taking up space and not pulling its weight? If so, turf it out. Be ruthless. We all have the habit of taking something out of the cupboard and putting it right back in. Well, here is a good rule of thumb. We don't subscribe to the two-year rule. We subscribe to the emotional intelligence rule. How do I feel when I put this piece of clothing on? Good, great, sexy, smart. If none of these, get rid of it. It was probably a mistake in the first place, and if you are honest with yourself, you will acknowledge that you never liked it and only wore it out of guilt that you spent so much. If everything looks wrong, why are you feeling this way? Maybe you need some help other than in your wardrobe. There is no shame in that!

Save anything that has a specific use, if they still fit, like jodhpurs, you never know, long woolly skirts, you may be invited to St Moritz on a long winter weekend, tweed jackets for jeans, coats that still look good as long as the shoulders are right, anything with fur or brocade. Save strange-shaped things that will always be a bit eccentric and throw out anything boring or truly shabby. They won't miraculously get better.

Throw out shoes that have damaged heels, that have crushed or misshapen toes, are too high or too low. Throw out the boots you bought in Italy that have a sentimental value but little else. They are dust gatherers. Give away, maybe to your best friend's daughter, something wonderful that you still can wear, but was suitable up until ten years ago. Give away things that are too big and too small, too long and too short. Altering them will lose their original line. Don't spend the money and don't bother. If you have five of the same colour trouser suits, keep the one you actually wear, don't fix the shoulders on the ones you hardly ever wear. Just bite the bullet and send them off to the second-hand shop or charity.

Now that we have cleared the decks, let's talk about what we can and do wear.

Black Beauty And Colour Me

You probably bought your first black dress when you were fourteen. It went with the black crayon you used to create existentialist eyes, à la Juliet Greco or Twiggy. Black was a reaction to pleated skirts, Shetland sweaters that scratched, knee socks, and lace-up shoes. Black was Kerouac's *On the Road*. It was forbidden books. It was a disguise for hips that were too upholstered with pizza and doughnuts. It was rebellion. It was stain-resistant and it made a statement. Black was Marlon Brando. Black was Peggy Lee. Black was night and Miles Davis. It was about the individual.

Think about it. Since what year was black no longer a rebellion for you? For the last thirty years black has been the colour of safety. It is always correct (except at a rodeo) and never lets you down. It can be draining but it has its uses. It is the building block of any woman's wardrobe, as long as she knows how to wear it. Chanel was the first to see its potential and its sexy charge. Her little black dresses were called 'poverty deluxe' by the sneering fashionistas of the time. They got it wrong. Black went on and on. Since then, regularly, the fashion press announces the demise of black. It is never true for us.

Black as a powerful societal statement started in the 1970s with a number of sociological phenomena, which were principally feminism, women's liberation and political correctness. Black is the post-Holocaust. Black is post-Hiroshima. Black is social guilt. Black is also gender-free. When we wear black, we indicate on a subliminal level that we understand the deeper issues in life. Or at least that is what it can mean. Now, when we wear black, we can be sending out a number of messages or NONE, because black is easy.

With the dilution of influence of the serious fashion magazine, its replacements being *Hello!* and *OK!*, there are no real guides for putting your look together. You simply cannot take your cue from celebrity culture. They follow their stylist's instructions. Black can represent a safe pair of hands, the kind of basic value system that eliminates differences of race, colour, creed, sex, and status. We can all wear black effectively with great style. Black can be like cooking. We all cook with the same ingredients. It is what you do with it that makes it great or bland, chopped liver or pâté de foie gras. For the artist in all of us, black is a blank canvas. Your accessories and attitude are the brushstrokes to make it special to you.

Black is chic at night because its darkness is always more mysterious and glamorous than colour.

Let's talk about the ubiquitous black suit, with trousers or skirt. You are going to the ballet, opera, or theatre with dinner after. You are sitting for a solid three hours in a small space, cramped, pressed on either side by a breathing warm body. The air conditioner is on full blast. Parts of you, like your feet and legs, are freezing, while your upper body and lungs are stifling. What to wear? Naturally, when you get up for a stroll round the bar you don't want to look wrinkled and crushed. Nor do you want to look sweaty and flushed. Because you are smart, you wear an Armani-look black trouser suit; it is comfortable, lightweight, and doesn't crumple. You may be coming from work, so you took a lace camisole in your bag to the office, ditched your white T-shirt, pulled, like a magician, out of the recesses of your handbag, a pretty citrine crystal necklace, tossed a dark grey and gold cashmere scarf over one shoulder and, presto, you look well dressed, a bit smart casual and very self-assured. (The choice of jewellery is vital. You may own beautiful pearls. Keep them for your jeans. The eccentric choice makes black young and cool.) This is the virtue of the simple black trouser suit. If you have chosen the skirt version, you will need to change from sensible shoes or boots to something more elegant, wearing either very sheer black tights or nude (Brazil by Falke is tops). Strappy silk sandals or slingbacks will dress you up and emphasise your legs. Remember, too, the lengthening effect of the beige shoe. Chanel did it with a little black toe to elongate the foot and leg.

We love the little black dress to bits but what are the options for us? We don't want something so formal, so severe, that it makes enormous demands. We want ease, elegance, and something flattering, not too rigid or too clingy. At the same time we must avoid the over-designed numbers which are everywhere with too many bells and whistles. For the trimmer woman, Prada does a line of classic black dresses with a bit of a twist every season. For the fuller body, Issey Miyake always carries a version of the black dress with some funkier connotations. Remember to wear interesting necklaces instead. Louise Kennedy does a lovely black lace number every season. Black lace will take you everywhere, anytime, except a football game. Never give one away. They are timeless. Black velvet is too heavy and hot. A black damask jacket with a bright silk lining, turned-up sleeves and jewelled buttons is a good look over long silk trousers and a turtleneck silk jersey sweater. Black sequinned dresses are a conundrum. They are lovely to look at on very young women, with just a pair of pearl or diamond stud earrings. On a mature woman, they must be made to the highest standard by a genius designer. Very little jewellery can be worn. You run the risk of looking overdone. And at the same time they have the incredible capacity to scream 'Dowager Duchess' at any woman over fifty. If you love shiny bits, buy a lightly beaded chiffon skirt to wear with a cashmere sweater. Or do the opposite with a T-shirt and a satin skirt. Kitten-heeled black silk shoes, dark sheer tights, and put in a little swing that says *décontracté* (relaxed elegance).

Favourite black things are well-cut trousers of all shapes: bootleg, straight cut, slightly flared, cigarette, cargo, wide with a somewhat lower waist. The best trousers come in miracle black nylon taffeta. You can virtually wipe the spots off them with a kitchen cloth. And since Miuccia Prada invented them, they are truly indispensable.

A black leather skirt combines well with cashmere, silk, and wool knits. Add some black suede boots or black suede court shoes. Add a white silk blouse and you are ready for any sartorial challenge. Beware of doing the entire leather look though, too dominatrix!

You must own a good-quality black leather jacket: the same rules of texture and variation apply. Try a black leather bomber jacket with a grey tweed A-line or straight skirt with a low-slung belt. Keep it very simple. Wear a black leather blazer, no studs please, with grey flannel or gabardine trousers or jeans, with a flowing white scarf.

Black polo-neck sweaters made of cashmere, cotton, silk or modal, with or without sleeves.

Black suede boots (not patent leather because the matt finish is classier-looking, unless again you are into *Belle de Jour*).

Black mid-heeled slingback shoes because they are less serious.

A sharp-cut calf-length cashmere coat. This is a basic for any woman going anywhere, anytime. It is like a fur coat. She can wear it over anything. Wear something light-coloured near the face though.

The opposite of black is white and they are interchangeable

Think of white as the colour of our now. Winter white, spring, summer, and autumn white.

If black is the basis of any seriously smart-looking woman's wardrobe, then white is its clever companion, whatever the season. I once wore a winter-white knitted coat with an off-white pleated silk/satin skirt, a black turtleneck sweater, and black suede ankle boots to a dinner honouring David Attenborough. Wear heavy white moleskin ottoman-cut trousers from Egg in London and a white T-shirt with a padded off-white silk jacket with Chloe beige shoes or camel boots. Heavy-weight but soft off-white denim trousers from Margaret Howell, with a white cotton shirt and a tobacco-coloured man-tailored coat. White wool sheath dresses substitute for the Little Black Dress. Keep white jeans, wide white flannel trousers with a white turtleneck in your wardrobe to wear with a navy coat or jacket. Never give away your white silk or linen shirts. They last forever, as long as they are never starched! Try a pair of loose, light gabardine navy trousers with belt loops and a white silky blouse and a pale grey cashmere shawl, narrow navy belt. Wear with white trainers. The best-looking are Stan

Smiths, or platform sneakers from Tod's. Big white and silver earrings and a few bangles of the same and you are dressed in CASUAL COMFORT for anything other than a ball. For a ball, long skirt or divided trousers, either printed or black, with the same white silk blouse (or lightweight turtleneck sweater) and pale high-heeled platform sandals. Loads of pearls, real or fake, interspersed with chains. Mademoiselle Chanel always advised wear your real jewels as fake and your fake as real. And mix them up.

― ― ― ― ― ― ―

Summer is white dresses. Silk, modal, cotton, linen, wide trousers, wide shorts, sarongs with fringes. Add a long silky jacket. Ralph Lauren always has one on hand. Just wear it with a tobacco leather belt, same colour sandals and a beige sweater or linen shawl around your shoulders and go to a tennis or cricket match in style.

Loose white linen or silk are comfortable and smart on the hottest days. Wear with beige espadrilles and a big silk scarf. On the hottest days, a charming fedora keeps you cool and cool-looking.

White bathing suits are a must, despite the thought that they make one look heavier. Nonsense. They make you look lighter as they disperse light. Cover with a white and blue pareo. Carry a large straw bag with your initials. Make sure the maillot has a lining and is not see through. A hat is a must. The white suit lifts your spirits and makes you feel young.

― ― ― ― ― ― ―

The most basic of whites is the humble T-shirt. Long-sleeved, short-sleeved, short, long, from James Perse, rag & bone, even H&M. The next must is the great white shirt (in Palm Beach, Valentina Kova). In London,

Egg and With Nothing Underneath. Sporty with or without long sleeves, always tuck up the sleeves a bit, to reveal wrists or further up. Wear with pale blue jeans either half tucked in or flowing. Wear your white shirt with the tails tied with a pair of white linen shorts. Narrow trousers, wide, it doesn't matter as long as you are comfortable, and that means relaxed, and relaxed means self-confident.

Navy

If black is rebellion and the avant-garde, navy is authority and comfort. We love navy. Ever since nanny pushed us in the pram wearing a navy gabardine raincoat with her little graduation badge and beret, we have been enamoured of navy blue. And don't forget the sailor suits we wore as pre-teens, and our gymslips. Think navy tweed coat with a little velvet collar. We look up to navy. Navy is someone reliable to watch over us. Navy is quality. Think naval captains. Airline pilots wear navy. Think the City. This is an authoritative colour with a formality and seriousness that makes us trust it and those who wear it. Think police commissioner. Think bank manager! Navy is a way of life. Just ask the smartly turned-out women of Geneva! They wouldn't think of a lunch without navy.

When we want to close a deal, hire someone, get our book published, chair a charity, meet the headmistress, we look to navy blue. Deepest navy is a winter wonder, spiced with colour. Spring has sprung when the first new navy blazers hit the rails, to wear with a mimosa yellow printed sleeveless blouse and dark jeans. Navy is a true friend.

If you have olive skin and dark hair, navy is your best colour. Black will drain you. Navy will give light and clarity to your skin. If you are fair: navy points up your limpid blue or green eyes. If you have dark skin, navy is less morbid than black and is the sharp alternative for a serious suit. Navy is less harsh, but still does the work of black. It tailors well and works in many fabrics. Think about a navy wool crepe dress and jacket with a bit of detail when you are off to a board meeting, or an Armani navy trouser suit with a crisp linen shirt, with drop pearl earrings and a fun brooch for lunch.

Try a Ralph Lauren pinstriped suit with trousers with high-heeled platform sandals in rusty red (from Ferragamo) with a white silk shirt, tucked in or half left out, and a bright polka-dotted red-and-white silk handkerchief stuffed in the breast pocket (available at Charvet in Paris or Turnbull and Asser, Jermyn Street). If handkerchiefs aren't your thing, what about a Victorian silver chain and locket with a dark belt with a silver buckle? Or a pile of baroque pearl necklaces (real or fake). Carry an off-white woven clutch bag.

This is fun, correct, elegant, and feminine and will go from boardroom to dinner. Wear the same look with a skirt for those occasions when you want to flash your legs. There's the fun contrast of sexy legs in high heels and a man-tailored shirt with an abundance of interesting accessories. If you like bows around your neck but realise how prissy they are, try instead a scarf folded like a four in hand tie. It's the male/female thing that makes us feel feminine. It is always chic to pair a navy suit with a French-style horizontal-striped T-shirt and navy Chanel-type flats. *Tres jolie, tres français.*

A navy reefer coat with narrow body and lapels goes over trousers and skirts. Wear a navy or black leather skirt with that gorgeous white silk blouse, tan belt, shoes and bag, sharp green gloves, a printed scarf, maybe tied around your head in the March winds, and you have a sleek instant suit. Wear with jeans, with grey flannel trousers, white or vanilla gabardines for a nautical twist. With those you can drag out your favourite flats or trainers.

If you can find a taffeta navy gypsy-style skirt, wear it everywhere with either a navy silk sleeveless shirt (Louise Kennedy has the best in London) or a fitted navy sweater. If you pair it with a white T-shirt and dark espadrilles it will go for lunch at the beach with a big sheltering navy straw hat! It will take you everywhere, as long as you have the right shoes. Valentino heels and gladiators are gorgeous and strike the right chic but unserious note.

Navy comes in any number of shades from the darkest black blue to mid marine blue... some bluer, some greener than others but always deep and mysterious. All great designers, past and present, Mainbocher, Chanel, Dior, St Laurent, Giorgio Armani, Jean Muir, Hardy Amies, used the juxtaposition of the masculine navy blue in jackets or suits to point up the extreme femininity that they adored.

Navy and white go together like gin and tonic, Adam and Eve. It's hard to imagine one without the other. So clean, so sharp, so appropriate. Imagine yourself on a yacht. Wear a navy sweater, white shorts or jeans and white ballet-style slippers with dangling pearl earrings. Try a long-sleeved striped T-shirt with navy or white baggy linen trousers and an orange cotton sweater knotted over your shoulders for dinner by the sea. Pin a coral red starfish brooch or a big enamel green frog on your shoulder or hip. Wear an orange plastic chain necklace just for fun. Put a fine white cotton polo shirt, white knee-length cotton skirt with a buttonless cardigan in navy cashmere or wool, pulled together with a gold safety pin dangling with a few red Bakelite cherries. Diana Vreeland would have approved. Put your personality into it. Experiment – as Cole Porter once wrote.

Navy blue is always summer and spring and gives you a change of pace as the season changes.

Colour me

In the 1970s some clever person started a successful business of colour counselling that put us all into categories: summer, winter, spring, and autumn. According to this treatise each season's woman was confined to a certain colour palette. 'Winter' was dark-haired and dark-skinned and her allocated colours were black, red, icy white, and bright blue. It was a nice idea, but one couldn't help but think that a fair-skinned brunette, otherwise known as 'Autumn', looked just as well in these tones. A pale, fragile blonde 'Spring' could only wear pastels. Redheads could only wear shades of green, olive, and rust. The laughing 'Summer' lady was confined to yellows and oranges. Where is the logic of this? If you colour consulted then, now is your time to give it up. You can wear all colours with an adjustment of make-up and the proper combining.

Think Yves St Laurent's use of bitter almond (a kind of musty pink) and avocado green, or chartreuse with burnt orange. Think Sonia Rykiel's hot pinks, dark greens, teal blues, and striped beige and navy sweaters. Think the sadly gone John Galliano's explosion of circus combinations. They brought joy! Today's flowered dresses have the same effect. Now, surely, we don't have to conform to one colour type in order to wear these shades. Did you need to consult with your colour consultant when you were tempted at Rive Gauche? No. Because you were buying a look, fashion, sexiness, innovation, and excitement. Your needs are no different today. You can use colour to enliven and enrich whatever you are wearing. Just be aware of the power of colour.

Some combinations are too lurid for us. Too bold colours can be demanding and unchic. We need to look for the half tones. St Laurent, RIP, was for ever and always putting together kind colours, perhaps because he was always designing for a grown-up woman. After all, he loved his mother.

We all love hot pink, chartreuse, sizzling tomato red, turquoise, and dazzling yellow. However, you might want to do it in moderation. Don't deny yourself, just learn to choose one or two things – a jacket, a coat, a skirt, a T-shirt, shoes – and leave it at that. Mix it with something a bit more neutral: white, khaki, ochre, beige, blue jeans. I personally love my navy outfits with red platform shoes from Ferragamo!

Otherwise you could look like the neon version of yourself. You can zap up your style with a bright blue or green handbag, or a wonderful printed scarf in gorgeous orange. Tie it around your neck or around your waist.

Another thought on colour. If you have found a wonderful multicolour sweater coat and it sings to you, bring it down by wearing it with jeans, khaki or chino trousers, grey sweat pants, and some fun boots, and pick out one of the colours for a casual bag. This is a great look for anyone. When you combine several complementary colours, the effect is neutral. For example, multicolour jacket, complementary colour bag and boots, blue jeans. Red shirt, green trousers, and white sandals and bag! It almost works like beige, but better.

Beige is wonderful but can be draining. Use blusher!

Jeans Are Not Just For Teens

Ah, the great jeans dilemma. I think a sociologist could probably write a learned treatise on the place that blue jeans have appropriated in our lives. I will attempt the short version.

Start with childhood. Jeans were for camp, in the outdoors sense. Jeans were sports, in the sneakers and games sense. Jeans were hiking. Jeans were heavy, dirty work, gardening, taking out the rubbish. Jeans were rebellion, *Rebel Without a Cause*. Jeans were slumming. You wore jeans when you went downtown to listen to jazz or went out for pizza on the wrong side of town. Jeans were the wrong guy that your father hated.

Think Marlon Brando in *The Wild One*. Jeans were for chopping off into shorts with fringed edges. In other words, jeans were for certain activities as well as expressing a social attitude, a fashionable post-war leftish solidarity with those who through no fault of their own did not belong to the bourgeoisie.

Jeans for us

- fringed
- bell shape
- SKINNY STRAIGHT
- WIDE
- capri cropped
- cropped flare
- INDIGO LINEN
- lace embroidery
- Tshirt capsleeves
- linen cropped shirt
- silk blouse Ruffle
- silk cashmere Sweater all colours

Then jeans became rock and roll, the anthem of the young. Flared, bell-bottomed, ripped, stained, bleached, patched, splattered, hip-hugging, and shrunk. You had to literally lie down on the floor to pull them on. Rock and roll made them sexy. From sexy they became erotic, with chains, belts, crosses, skulls and bones, bondage ties, and hooks. They have always been anti-establishment. Now they are not. They have assumed a category in our lives that has become so complex that it's hard to know why you wear them, how to wear them, and what it means when you do.

First, it's the YOUTH thing. When are we at our most rebellious? When we are young. And how long does that last? Well, in a society that only values youth, though the money still belongs to youth's elders, jeans are worn by those who profess to be endlessly young. And how do we differentiate between the still young and the wannabe young? Jeans manufacturers produce various items that declare the social differentiations radically. Only the young with the firmest golden-coloured flesh can successfully sport the very low slung, nearly pubic-area-baring jeans that emerged in the 1980s. The younger the wearer, the louder the message, and the lower they were slung. The suitable accoutrements to this very young style are cropped sweaters and T-shirts that reveal the more than mid-section, not to mention the ubiquitous belly button jewel or the less than tasteful tattoo. The low-slung jean has been done to death, looks frightful on everyone but the young and perfect, and is frightening on the less so. Today's high-rise version of the fashionable pair of jeans is even more complicated. You need a long, small waist, a pert bottom, and a small bosom. Even if you have exercised your body to perfection, had a tummy tuck and a buttock lift, your hands and face will probably give you away. Don't feel you have to do this.

Better to choose mid-rise as a compromise and why wear jeans at all? Are you doing heavy cleaning, getting under your car regularly, participating in country walks through piles of muck and barbed-wire fencing? Are you deathly afraid of being spotted as grown-up with a certain income?

Most of us are susceptible to the siren call of appearing young and able to compete sexually. Jeans become a complicated sexual and social statement and have to be analysed in those terms as well as a fashion statement.

Jeans can be and should be worn by a woman well over fifty, in fact forever, if she wants to. But there are a few rules to keep in mind. Jeans are tight. They should be snug. There is nothing more ageing and revealing of desperation than jeans cut to look like trousers. The baggy hip-hop look, so effective as a fabulous thumb-in-the-eye youth style is not for us. Take a good long look at yourself and be realistic. Your jeans must be cut for your shape. Consider the rear-end view first. That's what jeans are about – that and length of legs. Go to rag & bone and Nili Lotan, or any of your favourite shops, try every cut, see what suits you – narrow, bootleg, cropped, flared, straight- or wide-legged. Wear with heels or flats and have them hemmed if they are too long. Avoid the do-it-yourself look.

What to wear with your jeans

They are seasonal, of course, so in the summer wear a T-shirt or nice white linen shirt. A blazer, a leather jacket, preferably in a colour, or a cardigan maybe with a diamanté button. Make it feminine.

Pale washed-out blue jeans are good for the summer, worn with sandals and T-shirts, linen blouses and coral jewellery. NO HOLES please. Okay, maybe one strategically placed on a pocket. But it is amazing how fast chic little holes spread into massive rips and make you look like you have been through the bins at Oxfam. Wash your jeans and have them ironed properly or take them to the dry cleaner. But no creases, ever. Dirty, soiled, or sat out jeans are for artists, ditch diggers, rock stars, fifteen-year-olds, and rock climbers. Please, I know it is a bit cliché by now, but a good look is always a serious jacket or designer coat with your well-cut jeans and heels. Thinking sustainably, you might be able to find one of these at a very reasonable price in a vintage shop!

A slightly less predictable look is with an Indian print jacket, an interesting multicolour three-quarters jacket from Ermanno Scervino or Monsoon.

White jeans can be worn by anyone, as long as they are tailored to fit your shape. A favourite type comes from the brand 100% Capri. They are classic-cut and go with everything from a silk or linen shirt, a long swishy tunic, T-shirts, sweaters, the lot. They look wonderful with a long silk bathrobe-style coat, untied and flowing for a casual dinner by the water. They are also good with a navy sweater, espadrilles, some white beads and a white cotton hat, courtesy of that wonderful London shop Egg.

Black jeans

Now black jeans are a matter of taste. If you are an artist, a political commentator, an architect there is nothing better. If you love the look of black, and who doesn't, you wear them with a black turtleneck sweater and ankle boots. They are younger and more flattering than those old black trousers you keep in the cupboard for that one day a year you wear them. In order to brighten up the black-jeans look try teaming them with a Navajo-look silver concho shell belt. Of course they are impossible to find and could cost upwards of £2,500. Actually, Ralph Lauren has reissued his iconic concha belt, and though it is made of base metal now, not the silver original editions, they are decorative, stylish, and COOL.

As with everything else that you wear, update your jeans look from time to time. The newest leg or waist can modernise your look. Additionally, try to remember that black jeans can become tawdry-looking, whitened with wear, and droopy. As with all things, when they do, recycle them and buy new.

Speaking Of Blazers

kay, it's a cliché. You wore them to school, complete with badge. You hated them and longed for a pink angora sweater with diamanté straps. That was then. And this is now.

One indispensable building block of a stylish wardrobe, something you pull out again and again in the assurance that it will never let you down, is the navy blue or black (and even sometimes beige) blazer in wool, cashmere, silk, linen, cotton, velvet, or miracle fibre. This jacket hides figure flaws and as it does for men lends authority, builds an alternative body, and makes a timeless backdrop for a stunning piece of jewellery. Picture this. You are late for lunch, going to meet the designer who is working on a project for you. You want to look appropriate, not too overdone, nor underdone. Think grey flannel trousers, over ankle boots, black or tobacco, a pistachio-green body-skimming sweater, a dark navy slightly oversized blazer, big cameo brooch, fake or real, matching green cashmere scarf with fringe, and a pair of pretty suede wrist-length gloves from Paris. You are in charge. Not too serious, but well dressed, feminine, and in charge of yourself. You look like someone who can pay the bills.

Short and boxy blazers are good for skinny ladies. And they appear to lengthen legs. Long, narrow-waisted blazers disguise ample bosoms and wider hips.

You can wear a blazer with nothing on underneath except a lace bra, vest, or Chanel No. 5 and project a subtle erotic charge. This is a good chance to wear your pearls, a fabulous animal or diamond bow brooch in a sporty fun way.

If you wear your blazer with a simple white T-shirt and some playful gold or silver chains, you are saying relaxed, young, but smart.

Wear a navy-and-white polka-dot chiffon blouse with your blazer, pair it with a tapered knee-length grey flannel skirt, and you are talking business.

Don't be frightened of colour. Jennifer Tattanelli of Palm Beach has wonderful leather jackets that reek of style. They substitute for a blazer as they go with everything. I like mine with a longish pleated lace skirt for fun.

Bohemian Rhapsody

Forget your old ideas about wearing ethnic fabrics and jewellery. They can help you find an alternative self that is neither too tailored, plastic, overly conventional or wrenchingly formal, and, more importantly, original without costing the earth.

A good Italian friend, always fashionable, has found a number of sources with which she builds a wardrobe.

Chinese jackets, batik skirts, Tunisian jewellery, low-necked sweaters with big ethnic pieces, pashminas, ponchos, boots, hats, and scarves. She used to dress head to toe in Armani, and it was a great look in the 1980s before he became seduced by sparkling evening dresses. She would combine a smart slate blue herringbone tweed jacket with an interesting skirt or trouser. It always had a bit of dash, an odd brooch, an artificial flower, a dangling pair of earrings. She created her style. Then as her fashion sense evolved, I noticed her adding a note of the exotic. She would pair up a classic look with something from the Far East, either a jacket or a scarf. She combined the ordinary with colourful ethnic accessories to look unique. Another Latin friend always wears at night black skinny trousers with slightly chunky boots, an interesting long velvet jacket with a fur scarf on which she pins a giant jewelled lizard. She has a collection of antique silver tribal jewellery and yards of beads. She is not young, and not model-pretty, but she has the confidence to put together a dramatic look with a few good pieces. You can use this look yourself, but again there are some guidelines to follow.

— — — — — — —

Look for good quality. Is the design good? One of the problems can be that the fabrics are often made of cheap silk, and they look it.

— — — — — — —

Make sure the colours suit your skin. Again, traditional fabrics from the East tend to be harsher in colour and embroidery, so you must develop an eye for the more subtle hues. And though you should keep a keen eye on the media for trends and accessories, keep in mind that stylists generally are making photographs look good, not necessarily portraying a person living in the real world.

— — — — — — —

Be careful of so-called boho style. The young models in the fashion sections of newspapers and magazines, no more than nineteen years old, swathed in flowing chiffon, crepe de chine and mohair sweaters, dripping with fake crystal and generally done up like a bed in a small hotel in the country are styled by an expert. The model loaded down with layers of fabric plus hair extensions is a work of art, not a realistic example of what we could wear. There is little to be learned from these creations except DON'T TRY THIS AT HOME. Rule numero uno, keep it simple.

One shawl, one pair of dangling earrings. A pair of suede boots in a colour. A long, swirly skirt with a neat sweater and a pashmina. A long brocade coat. Not all together. That's for contemporary photographers, the Mert Alases and Marcus Piggotts of the world, to work out in the studio.

What constitutes the 'ethnic' look? Don't expect to find it in the big stores, although there are pop-ups here and there that feature Moroccan, Indian, Chinese, and Mexican designers, among others.

Again, most importantly: be careful of colours and textures. What looks good on a dark-haired and dark-eyed person is not always so great on a fair-skinned, light-eyed lady.

Think through how you would wear your new treasure. With black or grey trousers is easiest and most chic.

A little goes a long way. Smart women are always on the lookout for small shops that feature interesting designs and accessories.

The most important thing to keep in mind is that you are not doing a feature for *National Geographic*. You are dressing in a stylish way that indicates your aesthetic individuality and appreciation for these special things coming from a different culture.

At a recent charity event at an auction house, there was a great display of fashion error as well as what works. The hostess (*une femme d'un certain âge*, as the French would say) was wearing an update of her look of the last twenty years. Her blonde hair was in good shape, pulled discreetly back. She wore a black, well-cut 'smoking' suit and a pristine white satin blouse and looked proper and smart. She has always had style and she sticks to it. Several women of the same age were in the same look that they had adopted in the 1980s, but they were wearing the very same clothes! Fashion moves on. Shoulders, width of trousers, heel heights, everything changes subtly and with it your appropriateness or not. A jacket from 1993 can look frumpy despite its lasting value as a piece of warm clothing. But a touch of the exotic can bring things into perspective. One woman was wearing black bootlegged trousers, a black polo-necked silk jersey pullover and a black and silver short brocade Japanese kimono with some late 1930s jewellery. She looked chic and relaxed. Neither Eastern nor Western. Also of a certain age, she had taken a bohemian accent, paired it with some basic items and some good black satin shoes, mixed it with some period jewellery, and produced a look that was unique.

Tunics

Damask tunic

Silk shirt
Ottoman trousers

Jersey
Long tunic

Moroccan
caftan

Another woman appeared dressed as Nehru. She was a slight blonde woman, pleasant of look and manner. She wore a flowing beige silk tunic, leggings à la Indira Gandhi with a paisley shawl thrown over one shoulder. Her jewellery looked Indian as well. Only her shoes, which were matching moccasins, seemed out of context. She looked neither chic nor authentic. An Indian or Pakistani woman of the same age would look as if she were honouring her culture and background. A Western woman going for the full treatment looked as if she were trying out for a bit part in *A Passage to India*. However much you might adore Indian, Japanese, Chinese, Indonesian, African, Native American, Arabian nights, Mexican hat dancer, or Thai style, do not indulge in the whole outfit outside of a fancy-dress evening. The thing to remember is to use ethnic style as you would a spice. A little goes a long way. This is knowledge and sophistication, and a taste for another culture's treasures.

So where to look? Whenever you go on business or holiday to a far-flung place, look for local crafts: bags, belts, blouses, skirts, hats, jewellery, shoes. For example, in Mexico you can find beautiful embroidered shirts. These worn over a bathing suit or with jeans are stunning and fun. Carved bone necklaces or papier mâché bracelets can be charming especially if worn in numbers. Embroidered bags, tooled leather from a Moroccan souk, tie-dyed sarongs all have the look of authentic craft and can add something to the simplest, straightest trousers, jeans or T-shirt. Do not get sucked into the tourist trap. Everyone remembers fondly those Moroccan slippers in tobacco suede which we thought were so chic till we tried to walk around in them and looked like we had duck feet. Or the very expensive silk caftan with the artful macramé buttoning system that went the whole length of the garment. These chic little macramé buttons unbuttoned very easily but were impossible to rebutton without baby fingers. What a time-waster.

Beware the cheap carved soapstone trinkets so prevalent in Hong Kong and Singapore. What is valuable in the West is also valuable in the East. There is no substitute for quality, no matter where you visit.

There is a reason why tailoring is so expensive. Experience and expertise, not just a sewing machine, makes a wearable garment. Stick to accessories, carved jade, lacquer, lengths of fabric, or embroidered shawls, and add them to your existing neutral wardrobe. You want to look interesting, not confused.

The Joys Of Jewellery

What does jewellery really mean? What are we saying about ourselves when we deck our bodies – necks, wrists, not to mention fingers, toes, navels, ears, and waists – with jewels?

We can get a hint of their inner meaning by investigating the tribal aspects of jewellery. First of all, it is a repository of value. Indian women are given trousseaus of highly worked gold jewellery which they wear on their wedding day. It is an expression of their social value, an adornment, and indicates their status as part of a family in a traditional society. Italian women of a certain class are given good jewellery to wear as they marry, for much the same reasons: again, status, identity, self-esteem, an expression of worldly wealth, and adornment. North African women express their tribal ties and status within their families with beautiful designs in silver. American women flash their diamond solitaires. Ladies who lunch wear their jewels in part as a validation of their status as well as for the pleasure it gives them.

In other words, on the most basic level, whether you are Western or Eastern, jewellery sends a number of different messages, consciously or subliminally. Do you want to look interesting? Youth is gone, but beauty of a sort will linger. What makes you look young at heart if not body? Quirks, eccentricity, humour, individual taste, and a sense of your own identity. Your jewellery is a signalling device that you should be in charge of at all times. Search out new ideas. Break old habits before you adorn. Remember sometimes more is more! And sometimes less is more. It is all about YOU.

First, do go through your jewellery box and find some things that you have a special sentimental taste for. Keep those handy. You enjoy them and they make you feel special. If there are things you never wear, and wince when you see them, give to your daughters, if they will have them, or put away until such day as you can present them to your grandchildren or nieces. Or sell them to the highest bidder. Identify things that make you feel pretty. Wear them often. Earrings are always good. But as we get older we tend to feel that the size of the earring should vary inversely with the age of the person. During the day, smaller earrings or none at all are better. Dangling earrings are fun because they are the stuff of youth, swinging, dancing, sparkling, moving. Buy some good fun ones, they don't have to be real, just amusing, and move your head a bit, toss your hair, you will feel young. If you are the tailored type, wear antique diamond drop earrings during the day. If you love drama, buy gold earrings the size of dinner plates. They will light up your face. Vhernier make beautiful sporty creations that look good with anything.

— — — — — — —

Avoid wearing white pearls with your dressy clothes, the notable exception being with a man-tailored evening suit. They can be ageing. Kiki McDonough, a prominent London jeweller, says wear your best pearls with sweaters, jeans, and trousers. Wear coloured pearls and pearl and stone combos for dressing up. It is more unusual.

Do wear your creamy pearls with black sweater and trousers because they lend light to the face and will take you anywhere. Chokers are a bit ageing because their use is to cover the stringy neck! Show your neck proudly and wear your pearls in piles like the sainted Mademoiselle Chanel did. Fake with real. Even better, have them restrung in a modern way. A simple diamond or pearl line makes them more wearable. You can turn them back to front. If you have one with an Edwardian clasp, why not shorten the pearls and make it into a fabulous bracelet? You will wear it more often. Some favourite pieces are bracelets and brooches. They are more useful, adaptable, wearable, and transportable.

Anything amusing is youthful. The tasteful diamond brooch is not amusing. It could be elegant, expensive, and classy-looking but it is serious stuff. So if you should be so lucky to have a beautiful 1930s Cartier brooch, stick it on a sweater or a white cotton shirt. Wear it with grey flannel trousers and penny loafers. Pin it on a scarf. Put it on a collar. Make it relevant but relax your use of it.

Fake jewellery or as the French call it *fantaisie* can be very inspiring. The rules on fake are the following: a fabulous fake brooch on a lapel or coat or hat or even on a velvet bag is charming. Chanel made great pieces and you should look out for these in markets. Swarovski make good ones now. Beware of fakes that aspire to look real unless they replicate the ones you keep in the safe. You will feel confident that you have the real thing! That, however, isn't the point. The point is an expression of your taste, and the good designers of today are working in a realm of fantasy that gives any woman a lift. As long as she doesn't think that means a 12-carat zircon to pass as a real canary diamond, or ping-pong-sized plastic to ape South Sea pearls. There is a certain embarrassment in a fake trying to be real. There is a titillation to an out-and-out fraud. Try bright pink or big blue fake stones with matching scarves for fun.

— — — — — — —

Many of us have collections of good jewellery which we accumulated through the years. But remember that style changes even in classic things, and one good rule of thumb is what Chanel advocated decades ago. Wear real as if it were fake, wear fake as if it were real! In other words, wear your diamonds with jeans, and wear something decorative with evening clothes. Mix them together. Buy something crazy from time to time – a wonderful black crystal necklace, for example – and wear it with a ball dress instead of your serious pearl choker. There are fabulous Italian jewellers who make elegant mixtures, like the Vozza sisters and Angela Puttini in Capri. If you want to make an impression, a freshwater pearl necklace with a gigantic cameo will make a designer gown even more special. Conversely, nineteenth- and twentieth-century cushion-cut diamonds are appealing in a way that the perfect Harry Winston is not. Or just wear your one D-quality dazzler and go barefoot in the sand.

Antique jewellery or what your ancestors knew

It is a misunderstanding of antique jewellery to assume that it must be over 100 years old. For our purposes 'so-called' antique jewellery is beautifully designed and executed jewels made well into the twentieth century. What they have in common is a quality that cannot be duplicated today because we are all subject to the vagaries of the market, even at the level of top jewellery. Today's top jewellers, Cartier, Bulgari, Tiffany, for starters, are addressing a completely different mass market. Historically the top-priced jewellers were making wares for a sophisticated, elite, and very demanding customer. It was an expression of artistry at the highest level, and the buyer had a relationship with the jeweller. Today's jewellery is not modern in the same way that Cartier jewellery was modern in the 1920s when designers were inspired by the trends and cultural developments in art, music, and theatre. Very often today's designer jewels are made thematically so that they are identifiable. Witness the wonderful Serpentis of Bulgari.

The market is dominated by diamonds

Tennis bracelets, earrings and studs, diamond solitaires, pendants, eternity rings, and diamond-encrusted watches. They are very desirable in themselves as they are undemanding and go with everything, but they have little originality. We all love the Van Cleef look but you will see it in many manifestations, real, copies, and downright fake. However, you can find modern jewellers who will design something for you, but you must have a reasonably good idea of what their taste is, or you could be unpleasantly and expensively surprised. Rule: know thy jeweller.

This is why antique jewellery, and its interesting gems and settings, is so enticing and comparatively affordable. However, whether you already have a pile of it or are simply attracted to the endless displays at antique fairs and boutiques, antique jewellery can be a double-edged sword. It can be dowdy and aging or it can be amusing and piquant. It all depends on how you wear it. Many jewellers today specialise in signed jewels from the 1940s, 1950s, and 1960s. They are wonderful works of art, but might not suit your lifestyle or even the times we live in. Make sure that you can wear it casually as well as for the highlife. No point at this stage in life buying something that sits in the safe.

Wear coral and turquoise – there are fabulous examples from the 1940s – with your evening gowns instead of diamonds. Wear Georgian paste, mounted in gold, wear garnets, onyx, enamel, citrines, aquamarines, topaz, jet, and crystal.

Pick one beautiful thing and highlight it.

NO MATTER WHAT YOU HAVE, DON'T WEAR IT ALL AT ONCE.

Discipline yourself. The rule of less is more applies with everything.

In order to mix styles, you must spend a little time putting things together on yourself, looking in the mirror, seeing if the effect is a pleasing one. If in doubt, leave it out.

Do you feel like the best YOU? If you are more comfortable in those big earrings and a string of white South Sea pearls, by all means wear them. This is the alternative view. Practise with your brooch in front of the mirror. Vary its position and don't aim for the lapel every time.

In the vast cornucopia of antique and early twentieth-century jewellery, you must decide which adornments suit you best NOW, and this may alter with time and fashion. There are rings, earrings, bracelets, watches, necklaces, brooches, lockets and pendants, scarf rings, lorgnettes, tiaras, hair ornaments, buttons, belt buckles, seals, chains, collars, and chokers to choose from.

Be discerning. Choose what makes you look and feel enhanced and happy. It could be the most fabulous thing in the world but doesn't suit you or your life. As Diana Vreeland once brilliantly said, 'Style is rejection.'

Good choices

There has always been a desire for a beautiful cross or heart pendant. But what was a religious or sentimental motif is now a major fashion statement. Of course the Victorians did it first, and so why spend thousands on a mass-produced diamond cross at Cartier when you can find a unique piece at an antique jeweller with both value and unmatchable craftsmanship, in a broad choice of stones, at a lower price than any modern equivalent. Your friends will be pea green with envy. If you want to be sweet, share your source, hopefully a good reliable dealer, but they will never find the same piece. That is the beauty of period jewellery.

Special attention to be paid to the magic of the brooch. They come in many sizes and shapes. There are crescents, arrows, ribbons and bows, medallions, cameos, swords, flowers, hearts, crosses, fringes, animals, figures, and abstract shapes, etc. They come in precious metals and stones, as well as semi-precious, ivory, coral, turquoise, agate, granite, Bakelite, jet, enamel, amber, tortoiseshell, real hair, and pearls. Why not wear a Victorian seed pearl bow brooch at your throat instead of a necklace, or on a hat, or an enamelled and silver Liberty art nouveau brooch smack dab in the middle of your cashmere sweater. Put a brooch on a velvet handbag, on a silk or leather cord, or on a velvet ribbon. Wear your brooch on a hip pocket. Dangle it off a belt. Wear your brooch on a fur scarf, or any scarf for that matter. Wear them in pairs, either as clips on the lapels or together.

Keep your eye out in markets for brooches. They were out of style for years and now the cognoscenti know that they are back in. But the prices reflect the general public's lack of interest. By the way, if you want to pin a brooch on taffeta or a similar lightweight fabric, put a bit of material underneath to anchor it, to avoid damage.

Anti-Conformism

At this age, you are learning, at the height of your powers as an individual, another way of showing your independence as a thinker and stylist. You have logged onto history and romance. You have separated yourself from the madding crowd. You are suddenly a patron of the arts. You are recycling in the best sense. You are taking from the past and making something new and relevant, not to mention yourself. You are bringing standards and values to the eyes of others and translating from the past with new meaning in a way that a nice big rock cannot do. Hey, rocks are good, but they are not the only good.

Vintage

One of our most favourite bugbears fashion wise is this thing called 'vintage', equating something drinkable that has improved with age, with what are essentially old clothes. Of course, since the concept of sustainability vintage has acquired a political slant, as well as being a fashion resource.

But let's get this straight: for older women there is no such thing as vintage unless they are from the couture, were inherited from your mother or aunt, or are antique fabrics from Asia. Just the other day I had a ball with so-called vintage. A friend's daughter came round, tried on all my old cocktail dresses from the 1980s and walked away with an old Ungaro and a YSL Rive Gauche, pre-Tom Ford. She looked young, snappy, and cool. I also gave her a Bottega Veneta cocktail dress from the days of designer Martin Margiela. I had kept them, don't know why, because I had looked so great in them. But time had moved on and they were just old dresses for me, not vintage.

But why did vintage become popular in the first place? Sometime in the early 1990s, designers ran out of ideas. The minimalist style as promoted by Armani, Calvin Klein, and others had not only reduced fashion to its most basic components but discouraged the imagination of young design students. With the demise of the haute couture, the only way design students could find inspiration was by looking at vintage. With the death of wearable design inspired at the highest level, young women were wearing less fashion and more body ornament, and vintage was a reaction to this. Vintage was a return to femininity. On the retail end you had design phenomena like Voyage, old rubbish recycled into incredibly expensive tatty sweaters, and the second-hand clothes emporia. What came out of an Oxfam rag bag recycled with velvet ribbons and glitter led to searching through the racks of discards for cheaper but equally funky alternatives. There has always been a market for antique clothing, but the second-hand shops saw an opportunity and renamed their regurgitated fashion 'vintage'. When designers are bereft of ideas, recycle past glories without the technical and sociological implications and quality that the originals had, fashion moves to the past where there are qualities of production that provide elegance of fit and colour. It isn't surprising that some years ago at the Oscars, Julia Roberts showed up in an old Valentino dress.

The young and stylish immediately sensed the new zeitgeist and applied this sophisticated take on dress with a bit of twenty-first-century irony and thus vintage was born as a selling concept.

Is there a way that the mature woman can use this concept for herself? Yes, if you have a beautifully cut piece that was terribly expensive, went out of style the moment you bought it, and was put away for safe keeping, for example, a Hermès riding jacket in cashmere with a velvet collar and leather zipper tabs, or an evening gown made by a designer especially for you, a beaded jacket without shoulder pads, a long skirt, a fur coat or vest (unless you have developed an aversion). Old sweaters are never vintage. They are tat or fine for young girls. Give them to charity.

Anything from Chanel can be kept and re-introduced to the wardrobe only because there is a certain snobbery around old Chanel that basically says I had it before you even knew the location of the shop. However, if the threads are pulled and there are pills everywhere, sell it. Someone will buy it as vintage. The new Chanel has a different vibe, and you can do with that as you please.

Vintage can be very ageing, so watch out. Still, there is an exception to every rule, and one friend of ours has a trunkful of couture masterpieces given to her by her mother. Old Hartnell haute couture rejiggered, refitted, and properly pressed is the real thing, and if you have the body and attitude, the sense of self, an adventurous personality, and an appreciation for the handmade, and you can find it, do. The auction houses have occasional sales of couture, celebrity gowns, and vintage and it could be a good day out. Try The RealReal if you are desperate for an unused Hermès bag, if you crave it. But in our opinion, look for the new. Find a more current image and stick to it! And by the way, classic is the new radical!

Flesh

Look into the mirror and be fierce with yourself. There are a number of things you will see. First, you see the ghost of who you once were. That person is fresh-faced, has a toned body with a somewhat fuller shape. You have your youthful image of yourself, and it remains in your mind. Then there is that surprise that stares back at you; the result of living and ageing, the you of today. She has lines and a bit of deterioration. She may be well preserved, exercised, and dieted into a reasonable condition. She may have had a bit of work, Botox, fillers, a facelift. Her skin may have the faint lustre of someone on interminable HRT, but she is older, hopefully wiser, and a little shocked looking out at you. Then there is the reality of your naked body, top to toe, and you must decide how much you can show. We are still women. We have a sexuality that remains with us till the end. It is the eternal feminine. It is in our DNA and not to be denied. No matter what our age, we still retain our youthful hopes and dreams, at least from time to time. However, the question remains, how much do we put on display?

First, let us consider all the moving parts. Face, breasts, legs, shoulders, derriere, hands, neck, back, midriff, feet. Different body parts are commonly accepted erogenous zones in different eras.

During the Napoleonic era women wore little muslin dresses, wetted down (like a wet T-shirt contest) to show off their bosoms and legs. The Victorian erogenous zone was the waist, constricted by tight whalebone corsets. Chinese women's feet, bound at birth, were the ultimate turn-on for a Mandarin. Flappers in the 1920s showed their knees and back of the necks.

Breasts came back in the 1950s in an almost maternal way after WWII. Today the midriff and derriere are the elements of desire. No matter what the fashion, however, everything begins with the face.

Face facts

For the middle-aged woman, the issue is how to retain youthfulness, not youth.

Regarding make-up, take a long look at yourself. Let us assume that your skin is still reasonably clear and taut, you have good bone structure, pretty eyes, and a nice neck. However, you have changed. There is a papery fine look to some middle-aged and certainly older skin, or possibly a slightly orange-peel coarseness. It is drier. There is a teeny bit of droop and a lack of sharp focus that used to be there.

We need make-up, and the many brands that supply it are our best friends. Because we have lost colour, texture, and luminosity, going completely au natural is beyond us. Make-up can give us back the illusion of a healthy glow. You need certain tools and a palette of colours to achieve a fresher face. Take a trip to the best make-up department you know, look at several counters, talk to the assistants, but resist until you find what you think inspires you. At this point we don't need heavy make-up. Acne is usually a thing of the past. Do we want neon effects in eyeshadow or lipstick? No. We want earth colours, a bit of shine, moisture, and credibility. We want our skin to look smooth, even-toned, and healthy.

Start with the latest word in transformative moisturers. Every day the lab comes up with a new miracle. Some are better than others. Hyaluronic acid. Peptides, serums. Insist on testing before you buy. The assistant will give you a sample if she senses you are keen. Try a little on your hand before you take it. If it seems tacky, reject it. Good ones are: René Guinot (the Rolls-Royce), Chantecaille (infused with natural oils and rose petals), Sisley (aromatherapy based); 111Skin, and ESPA, ultra-light facial oils and moisturisers that smell of fresh herbs, Tula, Dermatologica, Cosmetics à la Carte.

After you have made this vital decision, you are on your way to choosing a foundation to even out your skin tone. You can lightly apply this foundation to the parts of your face that need it, always blending carefully with your fingertips, make-up brush, or a clean sponge. We like Chantecaille foundation, Chanel, and Giorgio Armani. Buy a matching concealer, either pencil or cream, for shadows under the eyes and around the mouth. Blend well or you will look like a panda. Laura Mercier does a good one as does Bobbi Brown.

Always use a portable mirror with a magnifying side and situate it in natural light so that you can see yourself properly. At night a good strong electric source will do. If you have very good skin an alternative to foundation is a tinted moisturiser which is lighter and more natural-looking. Very often these products have a sporty connotation. And try them out before paying out!

Are you too old to blush?

Most women look a bit washed out or sallow without some colour on their cheekbones. What kind of blusher should we use? If your skin is very dry the creamy types are better because they blend. Powder is good for an oilier skin or touch-ups. Again, use earthy shades, apricot, golden browns, bronzes. They should be sheer in texture. You don't want to look like a terracotta urn. Whatever your skin tones, today's brands have a full range, like Charlotte Tilbury, whose clever advertising shows a full palette of enticing choices.

Armani do excellent powders and liquids to give a tanned glow. Italians like their sun. English women are fairer, but a touch of light gold (Guerlain does a great range) gives sparkle. If your skin tone is truly pink or ruddy, use a correcting foundation and forget blusher.

The eyes have it

If you have always worn eye make-up, eyeliner, and mascara, by all means keep it up. We all need a bit of glamour especially as eyelashes may fade and thin out over time. Whole industries are devoted to false eyelashes that you can bat – if you like the idea. In the world of beauty, never say never, most of the time. However, fake eyelashes require upkeep. They are obvious, unless done by a genius, and can, at the most inconvenient times, fall out into your plate of pasta!

Always wear your mascara, black or brown, and separate the lashes with a brush. Use an eye shadow in a neutral tone. Stay off grey, it drains colour. Rather, choose from the taupe, slate, and coffee ranges, depending on the colour of your eyes. Chanel does an interesting colour called Rouge Noir, a dark shade of eyeliner that has a rosy tinge. It makes blue and green eyes more dramatic, and is velvety on dark eyes. Try not to wear waterproof mascara as it is hard to remove and may dislodge your natural eyelashes, which you need to preserve. If you are an avid swimmer, put your mascara on after your athletic endeavours. Keep cotton buds handy and remember less is more. Wash your brushes in shampoo often to keep them clean and bacteria free. We can learn a lot from French women. They seemingly wear little make-up, and that is because they learn how to apply it in a subtle way. Think of the ageless Catherine Deneuve and Fanny Ardant. Practice makes perfect, and if you are unhappy with your results, remove and start again with a light hand.

Brows

The problem with ageing is that most of us have plucked a bit too much through the years. Today's eyebrow shape is more natural, and sadly, sometimes those overly plucked eyebrows do not grow back. First step is to go to a pro and have a 'curated' shape, in other words, something easy to maintain and appropriate for your face. Then learn to maintain the shape by careful attention to strays. The current trend has been for eyebrows that look like batwings with heavy pencilling. This is not for us. However, eyebrows complement our eyes and frame them, making them seem larger. Thus some attention should be paid. If your brows were naturally dark, find a pencil that is a shade lighter. The same rule applies for lighter brows. Use brisk light strokes, in an upward direction, and a brush to blend. No tattoos. No heavy tints. There are, however, gel wands that can enhance your brows. The good news is that if you don't like the effect you have achieved the first time, remove and start again. No black as it gives a rather Groucho Marx appearance at his most furious. Keep a light touch.

Are you a lipstick collector?

Do you keep them, like fine wine? Guess what, the first step to a new look is to chuck most of them out.

Forget the dark browns. Turf the scarlets, dark plums, iridescent tangerines, mandarins, and mauves. Forget sugar pink, hot pink, and that awful pasty nude colour worn with a pencilled dark outline. Coromandel red is the Devil. Try instead browny pinks, rusty neutral reds, and browny mauves, with a bit of lip gloss. It may sound awful but a bit of bronzy glitter in lipstick is good. Estée Lauder has several beauties.

Dark lipstick emphasises facial hair, however sparse and bleached away, and tiny lines. Bright red lipstick gets on your teeth so must be tissued down to a mere suggestion. You could use a lip liner, delicately. Its magic is the suggestion of childish definition; it holds the colour and creates the illusion of fullness, as long as you can control your desire to paint on a new full mouth that goes in the direction of your nostrils. Try that Joan Crawford look in front of the bedroom mirror late at night, with a full pout, if you must. It is great for a nanosecond, but never go out this way.

The following should come with a warning sign: dermatological or surgical lip enhancement. Medical science has made this possible and we have seen versions that are successful as well as absurd. Discreet injections can provide a fuller lip. The same can be done with a tiny implant which will smooth out lip wrinkles and create a cushiony affect. As long as the practitioner is an artist, a reader of moods and emotions, there can be a pleasing result. But we have seen too many fish lips that do nothing to enhance the face. However, this is entirely up to the person and what works for you. Just consider that repetitive saw, LESS IS MORE.

Start your new lipstick collection at your favourite make-up counter for some flattering colours that will inspire you. You might try a gentle lip exfoliator to eliminate dryness and cracks. Lip balms smooth.

To gloss or not to gloss, that is the question. Gloss is a great enhancer if applied with discretion, just a dab. It is unnatural-looking in excess and simply functions to lessen the tenacity of your lipstick colour. Tissue off your lipstick leaving a trace of colour and then apply gloss. You could use a lip pencil on your lips instead for an even longer-lasting effect. Remember that we all make mistakes. That lip colour that looked so delicious at the make-up counter, when unveiled at home is a disaster. Too dark. Too light. Drying. Just bin it. Buy a pretty new compact. A woman of any age putting on lipstick and powder is a bit erotic so make the most of it.

Skin: the illusion of change

Facials

It's always a treat to have an expert facial. Gets rid of the cobwebs so to speak. However, a bad facial is like bad sex. Better to have none. Maybe you are not comfortable with people touching your skin. And if there is any excessive tugging or stretching it will do you no good at all. However, if you do like them, there are many expert practitioners out there. Ask your friends for recommendations. Cathiodermie and fruit acid peels benefit some skins enormously but be careful if you have sensitivities.

If you are keen to give yourself a facial to save money for new clothes, try the cleansers and masques by Clarins, René Guinot,

Lancôme, ESPA, Dermatologica, 111Skin. Before you buy anything, ask about perfume and additives in the products. Alas, many of us develop dermatitis as time goes on. Have the consultant do a casual analysis of your skin, and they will recommend one of their products. Be assured it will always be expensive. Otherwise, go home, whip up an egg yolk and olive oil, and it will probably have the same effect, just a little messier. Facials won't produce miracles, but they do have positive regenerative effects, appear to hold moisture in the skin and feel good for a day or two. The real benefits are relaxation, an uninterrupted rest on the treatment table, even a bit of a snooze, and a nice, rehabilitated feeling. If you have a regular treatment with someone you know, you can tell him or her your woes and it is almost as good as going to a shrink!

Exfoliation of body skin

A good washcloth, slightly rough, will rub off dead skin on your body. So will a loofah. A more pleasant and sweet-smelling way to accomplish much the same thing is to buy a commercial exfoliant product for the body and use it regularly. Salt, sugar, rice grain scrubs are now on the market, with every scent from fig, cucumber, or crème brûlée to seaweed and flowers. As you would use a moisturiser on your face, remember to do the same with your body. Clarins, Laura Mercier, and Coudray make wonderful body creams, not to mention products that are sold at the pharmacy that have no harmful additives and are far less expensive than the fashion-branded ones.

Run a bath, put a capful of oil under the tap (very good ones from ESPA, Aromatherapy Associates, Kneipp Herbal Bath). Brisk towelling afterward, not to mention body lotion, will provide glow and a sense of wellbeing.

By the way, if you are afraid of Lyme disease, Skin So Soft from Avon is a known tick deterrent. If you are planning to visit the American countryside sometime soon, or even Richmond Park, it's a must.

Teeth

Did you know that as we age our ability to keep our teeth clean naturally with our own saliva diminishes? Not to shock, but saliva gets thicker as we get older. Check your teeth in that very same mirror you use to powder your nose. Bleaching teeth is a popular new way to brighten your smile and is done at the dentist with laser light and topped up at home with bleaching trays. Floss regularly with Oral B, unwaxed, mint-flavoured tape, and use an electric toothbrush with a waterjet built in. Make friends with your dental hygienist because you will be seeing him/her four times a year.

Hair

This is not a hair consultancy. But clean well-cut hair, up-to-date roots, and attitude are a must.

Again, there are rules. Older hair needs to be lighter in tone. Don't go darker. Don't try to hang on to your original colour because you are not your original colour. Go to the best salon you can afford and talk to them. They want your business. Most good ones will be honest.

Bring in pictures, hard to find of course, because they are usually of fifteen-year-old models or photoshopped beauties with hair extensions. Don't be afraid to give your opinion. Ask questions and then relax.

Blonde or blonder is the easiest to go for but be careful because it can turn brassy, yellow, green, or even fall out.

It can look very cheap, which is why a first-rate salon is a must expense. Highlights in particular need skill if not artistry. The latest trend for highlights is to use a brush, over your tint, to highlight or darken some of your hairs. The long process of wrapping each strand in aluminium foil is not necessary for subtle variations in tone.

It is worth a trip to the big city for a consultation if you live out of town, for which you will be charged in some salons. If you have always coloured your hair, keep up with new products and looks, tweak it a bit from time to time. Discuss it with your colourist. Discuss it with your colourist. Alternatively, undyed grey hair can work really well on some women whose colouring is incredibly vivid, and they can do grey and white.

Products on less than perfect hair are transforming. Think hair wax, glosses, anti-frizz serums, deep conditioners, and sprays. All of these products give the illusion of healthy hair. And that means movement, silkiness, separate strands, not helmets of fixed-coloured cement. Every time you blow dry your hair you are damaging it. Therefore you must have a professional conditioning every so often. Use a deep conditioning product at home if you do your own hair. If your hair is kinky and you want it straight, throw out the old straighteners and invest in ceramic straighteners and the latest Dyson model. They will not damage the hair shaft and do not overheat. If your hair is straight, again lotions, mousses, gels, and thickeners all give body and volume. Go to your local pharmacy where there are many small brands that entice. Avoid the cheaper brands in the supermarket as they might dry and damage your hair. Use covered elastic bands if you pull your hair back – no cheap hair grips or clips because they pull your hair out and we cannot afford to lose a single strand unnecessarily. If it is practical, do cover your head when the occasional sunbeam might hit you, even in the city. The sun lightens natural hair colour and can dry out highlighted hair.

Haircuts

Having your hair cut can be one of life's most traumatic events. We can all remember going into a hairdresser in a mad mood and saying, 'Cut it off.' In our youth this usually happened after seeing a movie where the heroine was very gamine and had her hair point-cut, or as in the 1960s was cut geometrically. Vidal Sassoon launched thousands of young women with squared-off fringes and short back and sides. But the flappers of the 1920s did it first. In 'Bernice Bobs Her Hair', by F. Scott Fitzgerald, the eponymous heroine has her beautiful long hair cut off in a boyish bob in response to a dare by her mean and bitchy cousin. She contemplates her new shorn self in a mirror and sees that she has lost her womanly charm, which has been replaced by an androgynous one. She wreaks a terrible revenge on her cousin by chopping off her long thick blonde braid while she sleeps. In the last scene we see Bernice defiantly running out of her aunt's house, carrying a carelessly packed suitcase, in full moonlight, running for the train station. As she leaves the front porch, she hurls the severed braid against the door in defiance. Two things have happened here. Bernice has been shorn of traditional feminine values. She has lost something precious, and in its place gained a new kind of assertion and aggressiveness. A tentative self-confidence has been born – that she can renew herself, that she doesn't need her hair to become the person she wants to be. She is free.

And that is what most of us have tasted when we have made a radical decision to change our hairstyle, freeing ourselves, but also in a small sense inventing a new self. Without becoming overly intellectual about this, a new haircut is radicalising, in the sense that people notice it, respond to you in a different way, and may expect you to be a different kind of person.

After 9/11 Kaaren went to her hairdresser of fifteen years and said, 'I have always wanted short hair, cut it.' Usually he resisted when these impulses came upon her. This time he did not. Snip, snip, snip, off it all went. When it was over, she felt a little like Bernice. Freer. The response to it from her husband and everyone else was singular and had a most definite sexual dimension. Short hair was a boyish shock. It was gender play. Short hair was a challenge. It changed people's perceptions. She gained the attention of men she knew. Strangers approached her. She had restructured herself by changing her hair, and the response she got was not always a predictable one. She liked it, but it did not suit entirely who she felt she was. She found herself acting like a different person. She was over fifty. Within two years she had returned to her original length, with a bit of modern adjustment. She had felt uncomfortable as if a part of herself had been lost. Now, it can be just that, a part of yourself that you lose, OR it can be a paring away of excess baggage.

For example, if every day is a bad hair day, if it is limp and unresponsive to the many potions we are recommending, then maybe it is time to sharpen up and chop or insert a few extensions with some adhesive. Do not try this yourself at home. If it is wiry and ill-tempered and needs constant discipline at the hairdresser to get it smooth, maybe this too is the opportunity for a rethink, maybe grow it longer to be able to put it up or pull it back, maybe go even shorter! Maybe it needs a Kérastase straightening treatment.

Short hair requires a great deal of maintenance, but it can say something challenging and exciting about you. It has to be cut regularly. No lazy people need apply here, and if you colour it, your hair will need even more vigilance.

Long hair, when you have been used to a wash and wear haircut, requires a change of thinking as well.

———————

Whatever might tempt you, here are a few thoughts:

Very long hair on a middle-aged woman is possible if you have beautiful hair, and wear it in a distinctive style, off your shoulders and face. We have a friend whose beautiful long blonde hair flows down her back. It is her signature. She wears it tied, wound, braided, and in a long queue. She uses tortoiseshell, gold, silk, velvet, and pins to tie it back. A softer short look would suit her as well, but it would change what she considers part of her identity. It could be fun for a while, but maybe not for always. It depends on what you want to say about yourself and, ask any hairdresser, is a statement.

So after fifty be very careful about changing yourself radically. But also recognise that sometimes a change is necessary to reveal another dimension of yourself. Hair does grow back, as our mothers used to tell us when we arrived back from the salon, having hoped to have looked like Twiggy, but crying all the way as we realised we looked more like a shaved rabbit.

But if you are consistently aggravated by what you see on your head; if the thought of change occupies your conversation more than it should, then consider a serious change. It is a thought process akin to, 'Do you think I need to lose weight?' If you keep asking that question, it is reasonable to assume that you should. The same is true of a haircut. Your best friend won't tell you till after you have made the plunge, probably. Nine times out of ten they will tell you they liked it better before. But forget that. If this new haircut makes you feel younger and more powerful, then keep it. Become that new person. After all this is the process of evolution.

One little rule to follow. Short is good. Long is good as long as it is not flowing down your back à la 1965 in a Summer of Love recapitulation. Long is good if you are not keeping it in place with tiny diamante daisy clips. You are a grown woman, and if your hair is your glory, do keep it, but try to remember your dignity. Modified, medium-sized compromises are the most difficult to maintain. They are neither a statement nor a real change and they must be regularly cut to keep them sharp. However, if you yearn to experiment, you could either go digital and see what you will look like with a different style or colour, or just sit down to have a gin and tonic, relax by a pool, until the wave of discontent passes!

Let's talk about legs

Some cheeky man once said you should study the legs of your girlfriend's mother as they will be the last parts to go, and you get some kind of idea of what you are getting in the long term! Marriages today seem not to last as long, but if you can keep your legs looking good, maybe you will have a better chance! In this era there may still be some relevance to this observation as there is little one can do other than diet and exercise and this one must. Although recently there was an article about the latest physical augmentations by surgeons, the lengthening of legs! Shades of Fay Weldon's *The Life and Loves of a She-Devil*. Almost all the rest of us can be dealt with by science!

Naked legs are sexy if they are toned, tanned, shapely, shod in attractive shoes or sandals, and without blemish. No spots, varicose veins, dimples, wrinkles, dry spots, or bruises. The young can go without tights, wear very short skirts and shorts. The skin ages on the legs more slowly than on the face and hands, but a general rule of thumb for the over fifties is to wear tights, get St Tropez, have your dermatologist burn off spots, and do look at your skirt lengths with a gimlet eye. A tip we recommend is that if you are into short lengths, use Chanel CC coverage with a brush on your legs! Yes, leg make-up covers a multitude of sins. During WWII, ladies who could not get silk stockings powdered their legs and drew lines down the backs. The power of make-up can work everywhere. Limit the amount of leg you show, depending on your tough-minded assessment of how good aesthetically your pins are. Wear different-length skirts and trousers to accommodate this.

What do short skirts imply? Youth, sex, power. What do they imply for an older woman? They can mean trying too hard, lack of objectivity, foolishness, or great legs. If it is the latter, why not wear a short skirt? But there is short and then there is silly.

When we start talking about legs we inevitably are looking at the dressing we use most effectively to lengthen, slim, and augment. Colour, texture, weight of coverings, and shoes.

Tights and stockings

We love naked legs, with no socks, under trousers. A little powder in the shoes or boots and off you go. If you get very cold in winter, you can resort to socks, but we find them sexless though warm. Tights are an occupational hazard. There is no derriere definition with tights under trousers, so you do look a bit from the rear view as if you are wearing a tight girdle. Tights under skirts absolutely yes. Longer lines, warmer and smoother under clothes. There are two types for us – opaque and sheer. Opaque tights in black or dark grey create a long, elegant leg, a good silhouette, and generally are snag resistant. Avoid bright colours like red or blue, or you will look like a grouse. Opaque tights look best with high-heeled shoes because there is the contrast between sensible and sensual. Sheer tights in a nude colour matching your skin tones are feminine and grown up. Black sheers are for evening and the sheerer the better. Pale sheers imply nudity and that is attractive in itself. Too dark sheers make your legs look a funny colour and they show the first sign of a run. Only wear tan tights in the summer over a tan. To avoid at all costs, heavy denier flesh-coloured tights, especially with shiny Lycra. They look either like a surgical solution for varicose veins, or they draw attention with their dazzling highlights to every imperfection from bony or fat knees to less than delicate ankles. And please do not fall prey to the ghastly idea that stocking manufacturers put forth every so often, our pet peeve, patterned tights. At best, with tiny polka dots, they do nothing, at worst, with large meandering black fuzzy patterns, they make legs look grotesque. If you must indulge from time to time in a bit of folly, fishnet tights, freezing of course, can be sexy and cute in black or nude. But try to resist any other form of this particular type of retail hype.

If you are a committed garter belt woman (we are not), then we cannot advise you. Some women love the airiness of it. They find it freer and sexy. We, however, think it a throwback to corsets and foot binding. The garter belt is bulky, ruins the line of a snug skirt, includes the palaver of either bikini panties underneath or French knickers over. However, it's up to the individual. Maybe the sexy garter belt and matching accoutrements should be confined to the bedroom complete with satin mules with pom poms.

Feet

From legs we go to feet, which should be dealt with regularly by a chiropodist or a talented beautician. Rough skin and calluses should be smoothed away with regular treatment, not just for the appearance of beauty but for the health of the foot. There is hardly anything more ageing than scaly-looking feet with badly cared for nails and cuticles. In fact, your feet in open-toed sandals, beautiful, clean and smooth with a bright red polish, can be very feminine and young.

Bosoms, Etc.

Well, they say there are two kinds of men, bosom men and leg men. And which kind of woman are you? We believe in legs. Legs are kicky and fun. They dance, skip, jump, amble, and glide. What do bosoms do? They either sit there solidly or they bounce and jiggle. They are either solid or flabby. They come in several sizes which are variations on small, medium, and large, and depending on the message you wish to send you will either hide them or flash them.

There is nothing more ageing than crepey chest skin with mature embonpoint. Cleavage at the middle-aged and further stage is a bit of a conundrum. Women have breasts, so what else is new? BUT there is a way to have them, even somewhat older ones, and get the most out of them. First, be honest with yourself. How is your skin? Freckly, wrinkled, spotty, parchment-like or smooth and creamy? The bosoms themselves may be droopy, perky, massive, flat, saggy, baggy, or nifty.

This is something only you can decide. In order to get your best take on bosom status, try various bras, sweaters, blouses, and evening gowns that you have and decide whether you like what you see. But remember, plunging cleavage is blatant; it can be overwhelming, threatening, and young women do it better. Note: there is of course breast reduction and enhancement, but this is a job for you and a surgeon and not for a stylist.

Make sure your *poitrine* and your face go together. One may be older than the other and create an alarming contrast. We follow simple rules. If you have good shoulders, a good neck, and nice skin, a strapless top (or dress), cut straight across is youthful and complimentary. A plunging neckline is trying a bit too hard. Backless dresses are for the very perfect indeed. Frontless and backless are *de trop*, except in high summer in a resort where everyone is doing the same thing. The younger, better, smoother ones will be noticed first, and you will just be benefiting from the cool air. In addition, if you do dare to bare, by all means wear a little sweater, a tiny jacket, or a silk shawl over your shoulders. Do wear a bustier under a jacket. Do open a few shirt buttons, and make sure you have some pretty lace underneath. Unsupported breasts are okay if you are small, love your comfort, and don't mind looking a bit loose. If you are wearing a low-cut dress, not transparent, that is fitted to your body, and has a certain measure of lift, you can go without. We follow the Audrey Hepburn rule. You don't need to show anything much to be elegant, feminine, sexy, adorable, desirable, and charming. Modesty is a virtue in all things.

Time to talk brassieres

As a woman, in your lifetime, you have tried on hundreds of bras, from teenage training models to the Wonderbra, always desperately seeking a good fit. The perfect bra is supportive, comfortable, soft, flattering, uplifting, sexy, lacy, and doesn't cost the earth. Be assured that this bra does not exist, and you will have to compromise. If it is gorgeous, sexy, and fits, it will probably be expensive. And even then it may tug, pull, itch, and annoy. As a breast doctor put it recently, after menopause breast tissue turns more to fat. So even small-breasted women, especially those of you who have breast fed or jogged, need assistance.

Do you know what size you are? Women's breasts change all the time. One breast may be larger than the other. Get measured properly. Like mammograms this should be done annually. Different brands fit differently. Don't despair if you've suddenly been bumped up or down a size because the size of your back can often determine your cup size as well. 32 C is 34 B depending on the brand.

For us the best shape to aim for is a rounded natural shape, with a bit of uplift, not the coffee cup look that comes with padding. Now, anything that looks natural always takes more effort and costs more. So be prepared to spend a little more to get a good effect. A cheap bra gives you a pre-pressed, manipulated, rigid look that defies good clothes.

Are you wired?

Our breast doctors are non-committal about wires because there is some debate about whether they are a health hazard.

On the fashion front, however, we suggest a simple lightweight wire that does not bind but supports softly. Whether you have a bit of padding is up to you. But bras with thick pads, points, heavy straps, too many hooks, harsh colours, and liquid-filled inner pockets make a bad statement under clothes and should be avoided. You can afford to be a little wilder in the evening if you want a bosomy look with a bit of extra push up.

If you are a larger-breasted woman, do not be terrorised into buying a bra that makes you look three times your size. We don't care what the saleswoman says about correct fitting, insist on something that minimises and softens your look. How many times have we fallen for the 'proper fit' game and wound up with an expensive mistake if not two. Remember to always bring a T-shirt with you when trying on.

We love Hanro for comfort and youthful style. Try Eres, the best fitting off-the-peg bra around, but pricey. For flirty lacy show-off bras, you cannot beat La Perla, keeping in mind, however, that they are for smaller, not necessarily younger, people. Their styles are tantalising, but their shapes can be a bit unaccommodating. They are beautiful and come in wonderful colours and fabrics. Buy one and matching panties before you go on holiday.

There are of course good brands in the middle range, and they do very good versions of more expensive brands, but they can fall short on the comfort factor, because their fabrics by necessity are less luxurious. If you can tolerate a bit of discomfort, they are good value.

Tip: Never put your good bras in the washing machine, especially the ones with underwires. Wash in a little shampoo in the sink at night.

Camisoles and silky vests (aka undershirts)

What a sensual thing to wear to keep you warm and pretty. Pink, beige, taupe, peach, baby blue, and black, lace trimmed, worn under jackets, cardigans, and blazers as alternatives to blouses and T-shirts. Vests tucked in allow you to wear lower-cut jeans with a short sweater. No midriff showing, but a cute modern look. Your cleavage doesn't overwhelm, but you know it is there. A straight cut across the top shows pretty lace under the strictest suit. This is what Frenchwomen know from birth.

The midriff

We move now to the parts of the body that are always a problem for us. Let's start with the simplest. Unless you are a performer with a Cuban rhythm section, forget the midriff. Yes, you heard it. We know it has been fashion forward. Madonna did it, J Lo still does it. But it is so over now. And for us mature women it has been over for years. You may have a beautiful body, a midsection like a kettle drum, a six-pack, a wash board, but forget about it. This rule can be broken on a tropical beach, just you, the sand, the surf, your fellow sun worshippers, in a beautifully cut Eres bikini, plenty of factor 50, and a few frigate birds flying overhead. You just might manage it! Daytime or night time in the big city, utterly no a thousand times, no matter the provocation. This is the wrong erogenous zone for you.

The derriere

Every woman's biggest problem, the derriere, the nether regions, the sitting down, the bottom, the butt, whatever, let us not get rude. Has anyone of a certain age ever looked at themselves and said honestly, 'I love my rear-end view. I love my butt.'?

It would indeed be rare to hear a woman say to her husband or best friend when she is in the dressing room trying on a pair of trousers, or a trim skirt, 'Don't you think my bottom looks too small?' Have you ever been insecure because you thought your rear view looked insignificant? Because your bottom looked too narrow, too lean, too uplifted, too tight, too taut, too much like a pair of apricots? Ridiculous, except in Brazil where everyone has bottom implants. No matter how slim, how tall, how short, how old, how well preserved, it is a fact of life that women hate their rear ends. It is too fat, too round, too wide, too low slung, too pokey-outy, too flabby, too pocketed with cellulite, in other words, too BIG. So what to do with this thing that makes us crazy, that makes us insecure, that makes us grind our teeth at night, that launched a thousand diets and exercises, that created the market for girdles and corsets in the 1950s and control-top pantyhose since then, this thing that we hate and men love to pinch, fondle, grab, and generally admire, i.e., what an ass!

The cutest girls in the world hate their rears, so what hope have we? Well, help is on its way.

Take a deep breath and be brutal with yourself. Take a good long look in a rear-view mirror. Every older woman has dimples. Every older woman has a permanent crease under her cheeks. It looks enormous in the mirror, resting in all its bifurcated glory. Then look at the side view. Not so bad, probably. Try to remember that most people looking at you look at the front and sides. That is the good news. Okay, so your bottom is not a perfect peach with smooth skin, unblemished, and heart-shaped. It is actually a by-product of genes, age, gravity, and years of sitting on it. Imagine what your face would look like if it got the same wear and tear. So, what can you do about it?

You could exercise: water aerobics, Pilates, clench your buttocks regularly in a variety of dancer's exercises. You could diet and lose a bit of the excess. You can wear a supporting garment. And you can choose your clothes with some discretion and good sense.

Beyond bottoms

Trousers

It's okay to have a close fit over the buttocks. In fact, it is desirable to avoid middle-age bagginess in your jeans or trousers. But it is unforgiveable to have your trousers pull across the crotch and hips in a fanning effect. So don't pay so much attention to the rear end as to the way trousers fit from the waist to the lower hip. If that is smooth and properly tailored the back end will look neat and comely. This requires either trying on twenty pairs of trousers in a go and finding the exact fit for you, and/or trying the next size to accommodate the broadness in the beam and asking a seamstress to pin the excess at the waist and taper the back seam. Once you are properly fitted most of the aggravation will disappear as you contemplate your smooth unpuckered bottom view.

Most of our miseries come from bad fit. Skirts are much the same. I love straight skirts that taper to the knee. Even when they are totally unfashionable I wear them, usually to plaudits. They look great from front and rear, not because I have the perfect body, I don't, but because I pay attention to every angle in the mirror. I insist that the rear not be loose and baggy but utterly fit into the hollow of my back and fall closely over my hips. The waist should allow for breathing. I always ask a seamstress to make the waist slightly easier. Allows me to breathe and eat. Dresses present the same challenge. You almost never just walk into clothing. If there is no tailor on hand, and no one can pin it for you, don't buy it.

Words of advice on colour

I honestly don't think it matters what colour you wear as long as things are properly fitted to your body. Whatever your size, a good tailoring can provide a smooth, fluid line. Anyone can choose black every time, but my rule of thumb is the following. One colour, jacket and skirt, a suit for lack of a better word, deceives the eye and creates a sense of unity and good proportion.

Jackets

Long jackets cover it all if you are broad beamed. If your rear juts out, be careful that the bottom of the jacket doesn't pull across. A case again for a proper fitting. Long jackets with loose 'skirts', on the other hand, look sexless and ageing. Always try for a smooth fit.

A short jacket will emphasise the length of your legs, a medium-length jacket will cut through half of your derriere and reduce by half the size.

Patterns can assist you greatly

A patterned jacket on a plain skirt draws the eye upward. Conversely, if you feel big-bottomed avoid patterned fabrics. I love man-tailored suits in men's fabrics, a little pinstripe, a little Prince de Galles. It's elegant, plays the gender game in a nice way, and generally cuts well. Avoid large checks, broad stripes, big polka dots, or zig zigs (unless it's Missoni or Pucci, and you are less than a size 10).

— — — — — — —

When is the derriere a desirable and attractive focal point? For most of us, virtually never. But if you have a great body, good legs, great posture, were a former dancer and know how to pose and strut, are comfortable in a G-string, do wear black stovepipe trousers, a plain polo-necked sweater and kitten-heeled shoes, and remember to stand up straight and arch your back. Your bottom may become a joy for someone to remember.

Hands

I have never had nice hands. When I was twelve, I used to take red pistachio nut shells and glue them on my finger tips to give myself the illusion of having long raking finger nails. Later, I tried false nails with glue, which inevitably fell off in the middle of the soup course, often with an accompanying false eyelash. But that was the 1960s and I was young enough to blush and laugh about it. Also fake was a style. Fake is not a style when you are middle-aged.

My hands were always small and square, somewhat short-fingered with the most annoying flat, featureless fingernails. They were and remain weak, fragile, and always mid length, because whenever I let them grow longer they either tear or break off to the quick. If I have ever envied my friends for anything, and I would have loved to have been taller if only by an inch, it would be for their elegant, almond-shaped, translucent, healthy pink, strong-bodied nails.

Alas, fakes fall off, extensions encourage fungus growth and make it difficult to even scratch your nose without looking as if you could do open heart surgery with your nails alone. There are not to my knowledge plastic surgery procedures for nail augmentation or finger lengthening although we live in hope. But I do follow the primary rules for making my little problems look better, more elegant, and feminine.

First, as my mother or nanny always said, clean under your nails. I decided early on that if I couldn't have the hands that the model had in Revlon ads for Fire & Ice, or Cherries in the Snow nail polish, I would have clean, soft, no-nonsense, artist's hands. My little square hands would have expression and strength. My manicures would consist of rounded shapes and clear polish (as I am allergic to most colour pigments and frost effects). I would scrupulously keep them out of the sun, wear gloves in winter, and SPF factor 20 in the summer. No freckles or blotches for these artistic hands. I would wear gloves when I gardened, gloves when I drove, gloves for warmth in the cold weather, gloves for protection and affectation in the warm weather! I treated rings as an expression of my creativity and for years wore only a gold wedding band. My husband gave me an emerald and then on my thirty-sixth anniversary a lovely sapphire. I never take it off and I very rarely wear rings on both hands at once. I avoid small dinky rings that make my hands look crude. I avoid large flashy rings that draw too much attention to my short little digits. If I wear a ring, it has to be beautiful and in proportion to my hand.

I hold my hands like a dancer's. You can create a sense of grace and elegance with gestures. I wear chunky bracelets to show off my slim wrists and to make my squarish hands look more tapered. I don't fool myself into thinking I am a hand model and wear dark blood-red nail varnish. I don't file my nails square. I envy all women who can, who can have nails with diamonds embedded in them, or French manicures, but I have learned to reject. 'Know thyself, and then thou can'st be false to any woman', a paraphrase of The Bard. For the rest of you fortunate ladies out there with beautiful long, tapered hands, a word of advice. Keep your hands out of the sun if you can. There is nothing that looks older than brown freckled wrinkled hands. (Well, arthritis isn't a winner, but we can't help that.) Always keep your nails and cuticles trimmed and neat. Keep your nails the same length. Do not nurture one or two long ones when all the rest have broken off and are filed down. Follow suit.

Check your hands daily. For you lucky ones who can wear polish, I think dark red polish, except for the most magnificent nails for a special occasion, look like you are trying too hard. But a soft medium red or a pretty dark pink can be a nice accent when you are all dressed up. But for a youthful appearance, keep them shortish, polished clear or pale. Renew your hand lotion from the little tube in your handbag. Do wear gloves, long, short, or medium. They are so chic. But please not those old, soiled ones that you got from your Aunt Tilly when she died. They are not 'vintage' on you. They just look old. Give them to the next generation down. Always make sure your gloves fit snugly, another youthful touch, and that they are scrupulously clean. The best place in the world to buy gloves is on the Rue de Rivoli in Paris. They will show you every colour in the rainbow, fit you perfectly with your elbow perched on a little suede pillow, and send you on your way feeling chic, stylish, and saucy. Suede gloves are for me the ultimate expression of a woman's hands. They feel like the softest second skin, sensual to the touch, and look good in any colour. Good glove colours are always subtle even if they are the sharpest pink. And taking off a glove is one of the arts of seduction that never fails.

Scents And Sensuality

I have discussed flesh, all its component parts, so I might as well discuss the way your skin smells. And that brings me to perfume, one of the most complex things we can use to make us feel feminine, erotic, and above all still sexually viable. My first experience of perfume was probably as a child when my grandfather brought back Sortilege and Joy for my mother, Mary Chess and White Lilac for me from Paris. I felt terribly grown up. It was heady and romantic and I will always associate these scents with fur coats, artificial violets in a corsage, little satin pancake hats with veils, and high-heeled pointy-toed shoes. After nine years of age, perfume was a must and I never left home without it. Of course I went through some rather horrific stages, with strong-smelling stuff that reeked of potent unremovable ingredients, like Tabu. I loved it but it probably made others gag. A bit like the strongest Oud today!!

After I married, I met my husband's French aunt. She was a big woman with big hands, a big head, big hair, and not your shrinking violet. She was quite imperious and scared me to death most of the time. But when

I leant down to kiss her downy cheek and I inhaled the marvellous scents she wore, I would always experience intense pleasure. She wore only Guerlain, because as she said it was only made of natural things. She was utterly seductive, and perfume was as much part of her charm as the champagne and little canapes she served at cocktail time, the same ones for twenty-five years, in the tiny kitchen she had.

Perfume is part of the arsenal of seduction, of lifelong femininity, the sacredness of being female. Perfume is about being sexy and, in some very basic sense, powerful. It can be the essence of what you think about yourself. And for this reason I approach the subject with caution.

For me real perfume will always and forever be French. It is the foundation of every Frenchwoman's ideas about herself. It is rich and mysterious, floral and sophisticated. It says reams about your personality, your flaws, your strengths, what you feel about yourself, and it always does it in the most personal way, up close. For us, *les femmes d'un certain âge*, French perfume is a must, a necessity, not a choice. We can no longer come over as freshly scrubbed linen, or a newly mowed lawn. We are not a peach and parsley salad. We are not a cup of cappuccino with a dusting of mocha. We are not aftershave. We are not sandalwood. We are Bulgarian rose and tuberose. We are hyacinth and Chinese camellia. We are all the classic scents. We are sporty and we sport Hermès Hiris or Calèche. We are seductresses and we wear Mille, or Jolie Madame, or Bandit by Robert Piguet. We are modern and sceptical. We wear Chanel No. 19 or, even better, No. 22. We search out the old scents, Guerlain, Creed, *les senteurs et les gantiers* from the Rue des Capucines. You cannot smell our perfume three seats away in a restaurant. You have to sit right down next to us, whisper in our little shell-like ear and you get it full throttle. It is throaty, slightly whiskey-voiced, it confides its message. I love my black old-fashioned bottle of Arpege. I adore Fracas and Annick Goutal's Passion and La Violette. I adore Fig from Carthusia in Capri. I do not wear anything that smells like a fruit salad, cooking oil, food, leather, astringent, or motor oil.

I will not wear anything called Cool, Traction, Obsession, Ooze, Rush, Addiction (with the exception of the original Opium by the blessed Yves St Laurent), Therapy, Rapture, etc. Body parts are definitely out, armpits or lower. I do not want to be hit direct in the olfactories with the equivalent of a Mickey Finn. I want ease and *je ne sais quoi*. I want soft music, a bit of jazz, a twinge of sharp green to wake me up, a tiny touch of ginger to tweak my nerves, and a deep, dark sense of magic in my scent. And those are the originals, and they have few to equal them. There are perfume launches every day of the week, month and year. Companies spend millions on them. Most of them fall into categories. Some are good, like Carolina Herrera, which is mostly gardenia, but the rest are fashion, fads, and fall dead within a year. When I talk about perfume, I am talking about Mozart, Bach, Cole Porter, a couture Chanel suit, a Valentino ball dress. I am talking class. You are a grown-up now, and you have probably tried them all, from Jungle Gardenia when you were a kid to the latest one on the market, called, oh I don't know what, Brutality, or something. The classics are there for you. Stick to them.

Luxury

It amuses me that there is a so-called luxury industry. After all, the word luxury implies limited supply, artisan-produced, high standards, exclusivity, and elitism. How can you have an industry that supplies tens of thousands of luxury items. Is Louis Vuitton a luxury item? For many it is a cult, a fashion, something utilitarian, a status symbol, a desperate kind of trendiness, but luxury? Can you buy luxury at the Duty Free? Does luxury have a kind of timeless quality or is it subject to the shifting vagaries of supply and demand in the fashion business?

If I were to describe luxury for the grown-up, I think I would describe it as a kind of exquisite pleasure. If luxury is not mass production, fashion trend, ephemera, then what is it? Especially to us, the adult woman who has kept her inner child, who loves shiny new things, but has developed selectivity, taste, discernment, familiarity, and experience.

Luxury above all is a keen type of pleasure. It is knowing you have the best of something. We don't show our handmade silk bra and panties, but we know we have them on. There is a kind of secret intimacy about luxury. We turn our beautiful emerald solitaire inwards when we are on the street or cover it with gloves, but it is there on our finger, and we know it. We wear fur on the inside of a coat or trimmed discreetly on a beautiful designer coat or suit, maybe one made for us, and we know it gives us a sense of uniqueness.

Luxury is selfish. It doesn't share well, unless of course it is a half-pound of beluga. Luxury is selfish because it is for you. It is a kind of freedom to choose. You buy it because you can afford it, you have saved for it, sacrificed for it. You have it because someone bought it for you, thinking you were worth every penny.

Luxury is care. Most luxury items require a regimen of good care, whether it is cleaning, mending, polishing, laundering, ironing, folding, storing. If something is a luxury it cannot and should not be treated harshly. I hate seeing women carrying a Hermès bag in a careless, disrespectful way as if it meant nothing to them. That's a kind of mindless greed and arrogance that has nothing to do with luxury.

Luxury is limited. Oh, not that silly thing where the latest shoe at Prada has a waiting list. You don't have to put your name down on a list somewhere, although at Hermès it is vital. Luxury is something you find, discover, that few other people know about, and if they do they don't shout it out. Luxury is about the beautiful and sensual. Luxury is seductive, calls out to your psyche in some fundamental way. It speaks a universal language of desire. Luxury is a search for what ultimately satisfies aesthetically and sensually. So what are these luxury things?

The exquisite. Handmade, hand wrought, beautifully lined, soft and sweet to the touch, light of weight, flexible, full of charm, warmth, smoothness, polish, and elegance.

The finest leather in the most exclusive colours. What could be more luxurious than a golden yellow or soft pink Delvaux bag from Brussels, or a beautifully used Hermès Kelly in blue jeans blue? We love: a beautiful suede jacket in an unusual colour. Leather gloves from Paris in the palest shades of grey, green, yellow, or beige. Pale slingback shoes from Manolo Blahnik to be worn with everything. A soft woven wallet from Bottega Veneta with compartments.

Cashmere

There are probably more grades of cashmere than any of us can name, but the finest producers weave and knit from a grade that is distinguished by its feel, the way the dye takes, the way it falls, and its price. The stuff you find in a high street store, and there is no offence meant here, is simply not a luxury item. If you want a piece of luxury cashmere, the measurement is always feel. Most good manufacturers today are improving their designs so that good quality at Pringle or Barrie, for example, does not mean a boring twin set with a badly set neckline and a boxy fit. What could be more luxurious than a soft fleecy pair of black cashmere trousers to wear on an airplane with a comfortable cashmere tunic top. You look smart, expensively turned out, and correct. You are warm and comfortable. The essence of good dress of course is correctness in every situation, whether it is being dressed to the nines for a dinner at Harry's Bar, or in a cashmere sleep suit on a Boeing. Loro Piana has become the measuring yardstick for quality, but alas their prices reflect not just their quality but something else. Status. That is not what we talk about here, but if brand status is what turns your head, then by all means venture in and buy a terrific vest with mink trim. Good at Aspen or St Moritz, and on a trip to the Yukon.

Silk

Silk is a luxury item when it is good quality, heavy in weight, cut well and made into objects of desire, whether lingerie, dresses, blouses, or scarves. Silk is not a luxury item when it is a cheap grade, brightly dyed and stiff, made badly, and sold by the kilo.

Nothing wrong with that, but don't expect it to last.

In today's fashion world silk is distressed, ruched, bunched, cut, shrunk, and manipulated. It is woven, knitted, and is blended with other fibres. It is warm when it's cold and cool when it's hot. It is a natural air conditioner and does well in any climate depending on the weight. Louise Kennedy, a London- and Dublin-based designer, makes the most luxurious of silk blouses and they make an outfit! Put it with jeans and you are hip. Wear it with a pair of smart trousers and you are elegant. Under a suit you are ready for business. Handmade lace trim is a luxury on a silk nightgown. Hand embroidery is a luxury as long as it is fine and silky. One of the nicest things you can buy is a cashmere silk blend, which makes the prettiest dresses, holds its shape, and looks appropriate in any setting. You can find them at the wonderful N.Peal.

Linen

Linen is a fabric that has a romance and a status to it that goes beyond price. I would call it a luxury when used in bed sheets because you need a laundress to care for it. In clothing and handkerchiefs it is a luxurious necessity. The most obvious characteristic of good linen is that when it wrinkles, which all linens do, it wrinkles beautifully and in long loose lines and rumples in an elegant kind of Edwardian way. Think of the Raj. Linen dyes beautifully and is most luxurious in natural tones, off-white, saffron, beige, taupe, pale greens, milk chocolate, and toffee. It looks good in black and dead white. It looks cheesy in bright artificial shades. Leave the bright pinks, neon reds and electric blues to cotton which takes the colours better and has a crispness that complements a sharper tone.

Linen looks good loose and is at its most luxurious in loose drawstring trousers, flowing shirts, burnooses, caftans, flowing skirts, well-cut squarish tops, in woven sweaters, and delicate shawls. Good linen is expensive but lasts. The more it is washed the more beautiful it becomes. Keep it freshly laundered and out in the air as much as possible and it will be with you forever.

Cotton

Now you could say that cotton is cheap and cheerful and everyone uses it. But do they really? What we see in the fast fashion shops are cheaper grades and blends. For true luxury you must seek out specialty shops and brands and you would be amazed at the difference between a well-cut fine sea island cotton shirt and one from a mass market shop. The truly luxurious cotton dress, blouse, sweater, or trouser is fine to the touch, heavy of hand, smooth as butter and, whether close or loose woven, has a shape it keeps through endless launderings. It cuts well, looks sharp and crisp, takes detail well, and is endlessly useful. It is a fabric for all seasons but especially in bright colours in the spring and summer. What could be more luxurious than a beautifully cut white or sharp lime pique shift dress in the summer. Good cotton does not wrinkle. It keeps its shape and line and travels well. Cotton can be woven in a myriad of ways. Loose, tight, nubby, smooth, satiny, gauzy, opaque, see through. Judge it by the feel. Pure cotton will feel cool to the hand; blends will feel a bit tacky and rough. Spend the money and always choose a size that is a little loose in the hips for fewer wrinkles and a more elegant look.

Fur

Fur is a controversial thing for some. In the UK and the USA fur took on a moral dimension that put you either in one camp or another. Continental women seemed unconcerned. Now, unless you are seriously committed to moral ideas against eating or using the by-products of animals, fur has a neutral quality. Naturally if you are vegetarian or vegan, you will have your opinions and with that understanding, I would suggest you skip this section. In the current world view, the word sustainable comes to mind, and, oddly enough, fur is truly sustainable and lasts for decades. I am certainly sympathetic to the thought that animals for food and coverings should be raised with care and consideration. Cruelty to any living thing is unacceptable.

However, fur is a luxury. It is beautiful, it is warm — warmer than anything else other than an emergency thermal blanket. It makes an unequalled coat, cloak, jacket, lining, and in a cold climate there is nothing to compare. What about down? The more luxurious and light the fur the more expensive it is. Sable is the ultimate. Mink comes in a thousand shades and is bred for multiple uses. The most beautiful is so-called wild mink, but I won't dwell on this idea, since they aren't wild but are a species taken from the wild and farmed. The minks are developed for lightness and warmth.

Today they are woven, shredded, mixed with silk or leather, clipped, trimmed, and embroidered. There is no artificial furry fabric that comes close in terms of warmth, but you must make up your own mind about this.

Innovations

We must keep in mind that today's innovations are tomorrow's throwaways, but right now manufacturers are retrieving and recycling fibres and that is innovative but not to be confused with luxury.

Every so often the scientists develop something in the laboratories that comes under the category of luxury.

Ultrasuede in the 1970s was such an item. It looked like suede but washed like rubber. Everyone wanted it for suits and trousers. It was a luxury fashion item and very expensive. As it was produced more plentifully it became cheaper and lost its basic object of desire status. Now you can buy it for upholstery, and it is divine. But it is no longer a luxury item for you.

Microfibre was developed in the 1980s. It was warm, light, smooth to the touch, and made incredibly expensive rainwear. It is now commonplace in all manner of weather clothes and has passed into ordinary use, freely available, whether as fishing pants, weather apparel, hunting and climbing gear, ski clothes and the like. It is no longer considered a luxury, maybe a necessity, and in that sense is very desirable.

Nylon. The ultimate in common usage and common sense. There is a kind of strange irony that something discovered during World War II when silk was unavailable for stockings, and has been cheap and ubiquitous ever since, should be considered a luxury material. It is now, because of Prada. It is ultra-chic and dear. As Tumi luggage it is very expensive, thus luxurious, as well as indestructible, easy to clean, and impervious to the harms of travel. As a big Prada satchel it is both luxurious and utilitarian. So you can see where there is a bit of crossover in the idea of luxury.

A number of designers, in the 1980s and 1990s, notably Issey Miyake and Jil Sander, played with new and innovative ideas in fabrics. This can create a whole new kind of luxurious item. Something unique in look and feel. For example, Miyake produced a treated, woven cotton that stretches like wool, is as warm as wool, but has the lightness of cotton, as well as the easy care. However, ask if the textile can be worn in the rain!

I had a rather amusing tryst with a beautiful safari dress. I was on my way to California and packed what I thought was the ultimate luxury, a smartly cut beige silky dress, very tailored and chic. Of course by the time I unpacked my suitcase from that lengthy journey the said garment needed a press. I called for an iron at the Beverly Wilshire and proceeded to do my thing. Imagine my horror when I put it on the hanger and found that one side of the dress was longer than the other! In panic I pressed the other side again. It became shorter. Okay. So much for the elegant dress. And thank goodness it was far too cold that March in California to wear it anywhere. It is a misapprehension that California is warm. When I returned to London, I took it to a shop that handled the brand, and they kindly offered to fix it by adjusting the lining. When I got it back the other side had grown and the lining was pulling. I then called Paris, where I had bought it, and they suggested I FedEx it to them and they would fix it, no charge. How nice. It came back worse than ever. We FedExed it back again and pleaded for a refund. They were nice enough to finally accept the unacceptable and weakly commented that I shouldn't have ever attempted to iron it. So much for new fabrics, untested in the real world.

It certainly was a luxury since I had worn it exactly once!

Time is the ultimate luxury

We cannot buy time. But we can make time. We can create a space in our lives for quiet contemplation, for trying to discover what makes us happiest. And we can give time, give to those we love, give time to projects, give time to family and friends, give time to institutions, give time to ourselves. To renew, redress, and rehabilitate. We need time to think things through, resolve old problems, make new decisions, develop perspective. And in a fashion sense, we need time to make decisions about ourselves as women.

The ageing process is time passing. It can mean many things. It can mean giving up and giving in. Letting the weight pile on, the muscles sag. It can mean depression and loss of self-confidence. It can also mean new beginnings, and new assessment of your potential as a woman. It can mean a face lift, it can mean more purposeful exercise, it can mean more care of yourself both physically and spiritually. It can also mean a kind of selflessness where you have done the things you wanted to do for yourself and family and now have a whole new set of parameters. New interests, new hobbies, new work. The luxury of time is that while you still have it, you can use it for many purposes. And fashion and the development of a new look is one very amusing and important kind of interest. Your new look can keep you young and fun.

There is a woman in Nantucket who has always been active in the world of the theatre. Every year she shows up with a new hairdo, sometimes a new colour, including pink. She has been a boho, a grande dame and a punk, complete with Rod Stewart rooster haircut! She has discovered herself in a reinvented way and is always interesting to look at.

Sales

Ah, the lure of the sale. The Chanel invitation to spend in the sales arrives on stiff white card, expensively printed, and full of promise. The store shuts for a week, new stock is hidden away, and all the previous season's models are trotted out for the favoured customer who will arrive at least a day or two before to put aside the things she wants. If you have nothing else to do on a given day, a good sale at that level might yield some useful shoes, black trousers, a jacket that can be adjusted. Do not expect to see that wonderful coat you craved or a plain classic suit. They are either gone or hidden. By the way there really is only one chance to buy into the Chanel sale. Be prepared to make an immediate decision. There will be someone behind you waiting to grab it. Ideally all designers' stock would be made of biodegradable materials that disintegrate.

The chic boutique sales

Yes, do give them a try, although the same rules will apply. Most of the desirable things are gone and there is little worth having. But, again, the most practical things are the classics and well worth a trawl. An exception to this rule is to buy the strangely interesting thing you adored but it was so expensive you couldn't justify it at full price. It was either a shocking pink, or a spangled jacket, a once-in-a-while thing and at less than half price makes a fun fling. Specialty shops that sell cashmere sweaters are worth a visit, but you will find it frustrating because all the good things will be NEW and unavailable at sale price. I sometimes think the sales are designed, especially in London, to clear out the dross, and at the same time pique your interest in the new collections. I walked into Pucci the other day to look at some sale items, nothing that I could ever want, and there hanging right next to them was the new cruise collection, big as life. Naturally I tried on the new stuff and forgot all about a discounted multicoloured printed ski jacket. After all I am not going skiing. But spring will come in four months.

Coats

Coats are the best thing to buy at sales. Coats hardly ever change style and virtually never go out of fashion unless the shoulders change radically. Go out and look for camel hair, a navy cashmere chesterfield, a black belted coat with a fur collar, a sporty jacket with a fur lining at Loro Piana, the trench coat of the season at St Laurent. And if you should see something beautiful in leather in your size, grab it. They never change. If a shop specialises in jackets and trousers, by all means jump on your bike and get there early. Again, their stock is real, and you might find terrific wearable classics.

The after-Christmas sales are the most annoying to go to. You may find that special thing you just bought someone at full price, there at half.

Ignore the feeling of betrayal. And by the way, if you had waited you wouldn't have found them in the right size.

Only buy a larger or smaller size than you normally wear if the shop offers to do the alterations for you. Do not fall into the trap of taking it off to your little dry-cleaner man and find out that he doesn't have the skill to make it right.

Never buy anything with a damage or a stain, even if they swear up and down that it can be cleaned. Have them clean it first.

Never buy something because you see another woman trying it on and it really isn't something you would ever wear. More mistakes are made at sales than at any other time. It's fast, it's pressured, and the thought of saving money might be confusing. Take stock and take your time.

Sales can be good in a small shop where you have seen something you wanted and didn't feel like spending the money and there it suddenly is. However, if it is too high-fashion it will lose its fascination once the season is over and will qualify as an expensive folly.

I loathe most sales except for the sales of tights. Now that is where you find some real bargains.

The Cult Of The T-Shirt

We wonder what our mothers thought of *Vogue* magazine's announcement in the early 1970s that the homely white T-shirt was the building block of every woman's wardrobe. After all, theirs was a post-war generation of suits, tailored day outfits, line for line copies of French couture, little hats perched on the side of the head punctuated by a tiny feather, draped and shaped cocktail dresses with low Hollywood-inspired necklines, jewellery, stiletto heels, small impeccably cut handbags with clasps, immense swinging fur coats, and hostess gowns. Everyone wanted to look like Zsa Zsa Gabor.

Do you remember seeing that very issue, adorned with Lauren Hutton on the cover, big gap-toothed smile, swingy loose hair, blue jeans, white deck shoes, and the T-SHIRT?

She was the quintessential image of the post swinging sixties where the miniskirt and the Twiggy look took the imagination by the throat and replaced the WOMAN with the WOMAN CHILD. And we are still grappling with this.

However, what has emerged and remained with us is the lowly T-shirt, now elevated to an art, a cult, a way of life, an option, an essential part of the wardrobe. But what to do if you are no longer shaped like Twiggy or your curves are a little more than Beyoncé's? There are some rules to follow.

First and foremost and forever. NO LOGOS. If you are a female adult, presumably over fifty, there is absolutely no reason to ever wear a T-shirt with a message on it, unless, of course, you own shares in a bowling alley, a brewery, or are promoting your own T-shirt design business. To paraphrase Fran Lebowitz, an urbane *New Yorker* magazine writer who once stated in a highly amusing book called *Metropolitan Life*, 'If people don't want to listen to you, what makes you think they want to hear from your sweater?' The mere idea that we would want someone reading messages off our chests is absurd. So no T-shirts that say anything to do with hairstyles, drug abuse, sex, no brand names, no Gucci, no Prada, no cute sayings, no requests, no amusing aphorisms.

Only exceptions to the rule are on the beach, alone in your bedroom, lying down watching TV, or as an occasional ironic aside to your grown children, to let them know you are still conscious, a T-shirt that says THIS T-SHIRT DOESN'T RESPOND TO GRUNTS OR WHINES.

In the 1970s Kaaren was attached to her *Herald Tribune* T-shirt. It was blue, with the newspaper logo, and was given to her, even then, as an ironic statement. She had little money to spend on a wardrobe; it was the first jeans era. It made her feel like Jean Seberg from the film *Breathless* with Jean Paul Belmondo. It seemed counter-cultural, anti-establishment, and avant-garde. Despite the 1980s political activist/

designer Katherine Hamnett and her provocative logos, T-shirt literature has long since lost that kind of iconic value. Although the entire world wears these T-shirts there is no need for you to go there.

The white T-shirt rules

The white T-shirt is always appropriate, refers to youth, is a multi-tasker, goes with everything, can be worn day and night, and if properly cared for can last through any number of washings. It looks chic under a tailored suit. It works out. It gives an 'I don't care' insouciance to any combination and can actually make something starchy and middle-aged look much more 'with it'.

However, it must be cut impeccably for your body shape. If you have a bosom, no skin-tight T-shirts ever. You must try to find a shape that is cut close to the body, skims it, shows your shape, but does not bind you. Look for a weight of cotton that is not too transparent. Opaque white in a good cut is chic, especially with a bit of jewellery. Transparent is cheap-looking and tacky. Avoid ribbed effects as they maximise all the wrong things on every woman's shape. And stay away from anything fussy, like Dolce & Gabbana's corset T-shirts with hooks and eyes and strings falling about. These are expensive foolish wishful thinkings that belong to the celebrity set.

You can find a good white T-shirt in all price ranges. James Perse are the best. rag & bone are cut brilliantly. Fedeli at Trillion, Palm Beach are the Maserati of T-shirts.

Designer T-shirts are okay but often say less than intended. Agnes B. makes a great-shaped T-shirt that lasts forever but they become rough when washed. Too much Lycra should come with a warning. Too tight, washes badly, gets rough to the touch, shows every bulge, bunches up, and is uncomfortable and hot. Prada does T-shirts and like everything she does, they have both a good shape and a bit of wit, but they have logos galore. The last time I entered their emporium, they showed me a very nice T-shirt with a giant PRADA woven into it. I said, I will buy it if you pay me to advertise for you!

A round-necked T-shirt accommodates a necklace, pearls, or scarf. Avoid straight lines, à la boatnecks. They are too harsh. V necks are very pretty as long as they don't show too much cleavage, and they lengthen the line from neck to waist. If you are worried about the skin on your neck, wear a little chiffon or silk scarf. But do stop worrying. By the way, be careful what bra you wear if your bra is too transparent and you have a phobia about showing your nipples. Don't buy padded T-shirt bras that are shaped like coffee cups because they make you look twice your size, push everything above and to the sides, and basically negate the whole purpose of a smooth unencumbered line. Lycra does no favours outside of the gym. Flabby flesh under a tight T-shirt is not a pretty sight. But if you are small and lean, have a pert bosom and are in good shape, no matter what age, then a tight, trim, stretchy T-shirt is for you. However, NEVER, NO MATTER WHAT YOUR SIZE, wear an oversized T-shirt, not even in bed. Your husband or partner will turn away. They are shapeless and unflattering. They disguise nothing, even worn with leggings – in fact, leggings, unless worn on a paragon, are an insult to the beholder. Ali McGraw can still wear leggings. I met her in a hotel gym one year and it made me nearly weep about my inadequacies. The only exception is if you are working out at home alone or with your trainer.

Let's talk about arms

What do we do with them? Take a good look in the mirror, and do stop complaining, because it's possible to tone them up, keep them muscular, but accept that there is inevitable wear and tear. Skin gets loose, a bit crinkly, and underarm areas can be overflowing. Arms are genetically inherited from someone, and you can do fifty to one hundred triceps curls and you will still have some wrinkles and flab, although they can improve. Even Madonna has flab, poor dear. Recently I learned that the plastic surgeon's art extends to arms. Yes. They can be cut and sewn up like a torn pair of stockings. Legs too. It is all part of the rich tapestry of today.

Which brings us to sleeve lengths. When you look for a T-shirt wherever you go, cheap, expensive, middle market, you are looking at shape and sleeve length, sleeveless, cap, short-sleeved, slant-sleeved, tight-sleeved, three-quarters sleeve, long sleeve. If you don't like your arms, you have some choices. You could buy a sleeveless or short-sleeved T-shirt and wear it under your jackets or sweaters or open shirt. And it will allow comfortable movement, and it will be chic. If you want to wear sleeveless in summer, liberate yourself and just do it. No one is scrutinising you. If you are overly concerned, throw a smart gauzy scarf over your shoulders and walk tall. If you want to wear the T-shirt look, without a jacket or any of the above, the three-quarters sleeve, if you can find it, or the long sleeve, pushed up to the elbow is the best. You show off your watch, your bracelets, and forearms. Wrists are pretty, and even more attractive if you have a good manicure and a pretty bracelet. (The sainted Jean Muir of our youth always emphasised the wrists by cutting sleeve lengths just that little bit short.)

The T-shirt subset

So far we have only discussed the white T-shirt because it is the best, the most useful, the easiest to keep clean and the most enhancing to the skin. However, you might consider other colour options from time to time.

Big rules here

Black is good because it is city, it doesn't show grime, it looks good with everything, it's minimising and chic. Good with all kinds of ethnic accessories, dresses up and dresses down. Wash by hand with care to avoid fading. Best brand: Margaret Howell.

— — — — — — —

Navy blue. Good but not for everyone. Looks best when you have some colour in your face. Deadly when you are pale. John Smedley makes beautiful cotton and merino wool blends.

— — — — — — —

Khaki. Good colour for virtually everyone, brings out the pink in your skin, looks interesting. Goes well with white, black, red, and is a basic travel colour. Wear a khaki T-shirt with a pair of beige cargo trousers, linen drawstring pants, white jeans, black silk palazzos, wrap-around jersey, or linen skirt. Khaki is great in the summer.

— — — — — — —

Forget bland *beige*, white is better.

— — — — — — —

Pastels. Yes, if worn in the South of France or Italy at a smart resort with matching-coloured, beautifully cut jeans, or plain linen or cotton capri pants. Choose the pastel shade that looks best on you and wear it very simply, with flat sandals, no jewellery, and a straw bag. But remember, white is always better.

Strong solid colours... absolutely under no circumstances do you go there, except tangerine or orange, which bring light and colour to the face. Bright T-shirts wash badly, lose their colour immediately and are harsh. No patterns, stripes, dots, opticals, floral sprigs. One notable exception: the Pucci silk T-shirt. No jewellery, little make-up, flat shoes, a hat, white capri trousers and fun.

Working Women Of A Certain Age

Years ago I was in downtown NYC, and I do mean downtown, on Avenue A, in the Lower East Side, watching my thirty-something-year-old daughter being fitted for a wedding dress. The designer draped and pinned and my handsome dark-eyed, dark-haired daughter, all five foot eight inches of her, looked gloriously feminine. However, it took ages to get the concept right and approved and there I was twiddling my thumbs and feeling extraneous. There was another woman there with her daughter as well, with pretty features, freckly skin, and nice dark silky hair. We started to talk as we waited, and I asked her if she minded my asking her a few questions on fashion. As we started to discuss the fashion industry and their failure to meet a middle-aged woman's demands I was struck by the notion that I hadn't dealt with all the women out there whose needs were professional. My subject was a school administrator out on Long Island, and she dressed every day for an office, for meetings, for conferences, in other words seriously. And she too said, without any hesitation, there simply wasn't enough out there. She felt she couldn't wear trousers, preferred skirts, but there was little choice and what there was on offer was dull. She named a few manufacturers that she preferred, Max Mara being one. I asked her what she wanted to look like, and her answer was simple. Serious, but feminine, youngish but not young, attractive without overt sexuality. It set me to thinking. Here we have devised all these rules and ideas about creating your own look with accessories, jewellery, and attitude, but many women need something to wear that is attractive, functional, and makes them feel good at the office!

I was out looking in the shops with another friend who is a professional PR woman, and her complaints were the same: I cannot wear most things to a business meeting, nor do they have the flexibility to look good both day and evening. So many professional women need to make the transition from the boardroom to the dining room with little time in between, not to mention packing space. The common complaint was that there weren't interesting jackets and skirts, the cuts were dreary and masculine, fabrics cheap, details non-existent. We have all seen professional working women on planes and trains, grabbing their meals on the run, between family obligations, dressed in the tell-tale dark shapeless suit with sensible shoes and heavy-gauge shiny nylon tights. Despite the popular perception of career women, à la *Sex and the City*, or the stay-at-home worker in leggings and a sweatshirt in front of the Zoom, the average working woman is not racing for trains or taxis in her Manolos, braless in a low see-through wrap-around blouson. She is commuting between cities, immersed in her laptop and paperwork, trying not to be overwhelmed by fatigue when she arrives for her meetings. She isn't wearing silk combat trousers and a clingy top. She is not wearing trousers that pool over her trainers and an oversize waxed jacket. She looks pretty buttoned up and practical. What can she do to brighten up her wardrobe without bringing unwanted emphasis to her wardrobe instead of her work?

The rules of belts, scarves, jewellery, make-up, and accessories apply as much to her as to the non-career woman. Just less.

For example, look at the Italian designers in your local department stores. They tend to emphasise tailoring, dresses, jackets, or coats. You can escape from navy blue, black, grey, and brown with neutrals, beiges, and taupes, but what do you do to lighten and brighten your look? Too much expensive-looking jewellery sends out a counterproductive message. After all, work is about earning. You never want to look more prosperous than your boss! I can remember being caught looking in a shop window when I was a young writer on a rather dreary make-up account and running into the department head who took a good long look at the fur-trimmed coat I was wearing (it was my day off a week as a working mother) and wondered what I was doing in that neighbourhood. It hadn't occurred to him that my husband's status was of managing director of a company and he, himself, was several levels below in the management hierarchy. It was the bad old days, and I can tell you it didn't do my career a bit of good. I was moved laterally shortly thereafter into catalogue work. Ugh. On the other hand, you want to look smart and capable and have a bit of womanly charm.

Some tips

With a masculine-cut suit, have it tailored closer to your body if you can, with an indication of a waist.

Though you do not want to wear a short skirt, always opt for the trim or pencil-line skirt that hits or is half inch to two inches below the knee. Not a mini, not a micro, but still a bit of an indication that you have legs, and you like them.

Look for shoes you can walk in, and as you get older, very high heels are tiring all day long, but opt for a slimmer heel, with a low throat to the shoe. Try slingbacks for a change or suede ankle boots. The trend today towards court shoes with thick heels is a good one for walking whilst preserving a feminine twist.

We all know about the trainer/sneaker phenomenon. By all means if you are walking to work, wear them, but tuck your heels in your carryall. A must.

Blouses are an instant formula for dressing things up and creating an elegant and ladylike impression, especially if they are chiffon, silky, and are just an indication of a body beneath. Do avoid like the plague that thing that Donna Karan invented in the 1970s called The Body. It seemed such a good idea at the time: a tight, snug, low-necked top that snapped under the crotch. What could be less comfortable? An iron maiden, maybe a truss. They are impractical, make bulges on the side and, worse, they neither lift the bosom or flatter, more like flatten and poke your arm flab out appreciably. It's a no-go after thirty.

Though I love sweaters, T-shirts, and bare skin, for the working woman a pretty off-white silk, or black chiffon blouse can be dressed up after five with a bit of extra make-up, a bracelet or two and dangling earrings.

Earrings are authoritative. Why? Take my word for it. But for the office, they should be button earrings, close to the face, not small, not the size of dinner plates, but in flattering stones, pearls, or metal. Unless of course you are an art gallery owner, whereupon the bigger the dangles the better! Earrings are for lawyers, businesswomen, doctors, consultants. They add focus and seriousness to any outfit. Brooches are serious. Bracelets and watches are serious. Elaborate necklaces are not. Madeleine Albright, the former US Secretary of State, wore a suitably themed brooch wherever she went in the world. They were her fashion calling cards.

Working women can wear colour!

Yes. Just avoid too much of it in a single dose. Though I love the idea of a red suit, a red jacket and a tobacco-coloured or grey skirt is better. Red is a powerful, stimulating colour, but all over is perhaps a little too much for a work environment. Stick to colours and tones that make you feel confident. If you are doing business in Palm Beach, go for lighter and brighter, but still keeping things a bit conservative.

Patterns can be fun, and they are featured everywhere these days, keeping in mind that small patterns are very flattering, and big patterns shout a bit too much. Less is always more.

Knitted suits can be comfortable, great for travel, and feminine, but they must be well-cut and not baggy. There's nothing worse than a bagged, sagged-out back-end view of a women in a knitted or jersey suit. St. John makes lovely business suits but keep to the simple ones and accessorise carefully. Smart shoes, great handbag, and a pretty shawl.

The Gravity Of Bathing Suits

The bathing suit presents a number of problems as the body ages, principally its tendency to fall south. At the same time it would be a bit much to wear Lycra tights under a one-piece swimsuit, though we have seen it done in the South of France sported by a middle-aged woman recovering from a very comprehensive plastic surgery programme. It was said, with not absolute kindness, that the tights were there to keep the leg and buttock lifts in place. It was impractical for the pool, but she seemed to enjoy posing.

Barring such extreme measures, it is inevitable that what we are at fifty plus is not what we were at twenty, thirty, or even forty. We may be fit, strong, and indeed many of us look toned and terrific under normal circumstances, but the bathing suit is the test of our self-confidence.

First the skin. It is a little more slack. Its texture has perhaps roughened a bit, there are veins, there are little brown spotty flaws, the space between the thighs has either bowed a bit or filled in. Yes, you get the picture. That body beautiful that was your joy at the beach or pool, that was certain to get admiring glances has become just another collection of flesh and bone and is no longer pulling the right attention. Not to despair because everything is attitude and mystery now. First the attitude. We may no longer be pulchritudinous perfection, but we are still women. We have bosoms, we have rears, we have legs.

The mystery is who we are and how we reveal ourselves. If you are so out of shape that you feel you daren't show yourself, you may be right. Now is the time to invest in some elegant loose linen drawstring trousers, a filmy top, a large straw hat, and prepare to lounge languorously under an umbrella with large dark sunglasses, bright lipstick, a good book, and your drawing pad. Otherwise, if you think you are in good shape, here is some advice.

Have some pale St Tropez tan applied at a good local beautician before you take off for the beach. There are many home applications but alas one does look a bit jaundiced with most. The point of the St Tropez is to have a light tan on your body and face for the beginning of the holiday, so that your tiny veins and imperfections are veiled with healthy colour. Don't forget the suntan lotion though, as the St Tropez does not protect you from the rays. If you are a darker complexion, remember that you can burn as much as your paler cousins. Always apply between 30 and 50 SPF.

Do buy a new swimming costume, because the elastic loosens and leaves gaps when you sit down, and the chlorine from season to season bleaches out the colour if only infinitesimally. Bathing suits age even faster than we do. Turf out any old suits, no matter how much you once loved them. They will do you no favours.

Go to a good department store or specialty shop and try on an assortment. Wear tiny panties and take off your tights. Yes, it's a struggle and they may run, but it will be worth it. You will get the bad news and the good news and with some painful truths you may find a model that flatters you. Bathing suits are very body specific, and one cut may flatter and another may destroy. The goal is a sculpted shape with a firm body and long-legged look.

There are many other fine manufacturers to suit all kinds of bodies. Missoni, Fisch, Form and Fold, Eres and La Perla make glamorous bikinis and swimsuits which have some bra support.

Calvin Klein and Speedo make great sporty one-piece suits intended for serious swimming but they have little construction within.

Gottex is the middle-aged woman's alternative to Prozac. This range is very comprehensive in its approach to figure flaws, midriff bloat, derriere spread, and general flab. You can also head for Lululemon.

In the dressing room, look at every part of your body, including breasts, back, sides, and underarms. Look at your legs, thighs, and backs of knees. Be honest with yourself, but also give yourself a break. You don't have to be perfect.

As you try on each suit, check the fit, length, and support factors.

Always try to have an element of comfort. If it is constantly sliding upwards or pulling down, it won't get any better walking along the poolside.

We all have favourite colours. Surprisingly, white can be very flattering. White bikinis and one-piece suits look as good with pale skin as with dark and have a summery sexiness to them without being too overt. It's the transparency thing, the idea that there is flesh underneath, even if it is modestly lined. Depending on the style, white suits most bodies. We love white because it is clean and sharp and is perennially stylish. It says fresh air and bracing waves.

We love aquamarine, Gitane blue, lavender, rose, chartreuse, tomato red, and tangerine. These are hot-weather colours full of vitality. They look good with a tan, real or fake. There is nothing more attention-getting and flattering.

We have weaned ourselves away from black bathing suits. Now all of us have a black bathing suit, but have you ever stopped to consider how utterly dull they really are? You might think you were hiding your deficiencies but black usually draws attention and does exactly the opposite. Instead of giving off colourful beams, it says dark and dreary. The more there is of this heavy blackness, the sadder you look. It is obvious that you are hiding something. So free yourself of the illusion that black bathing suits minimise and flatter. They are no fun at all.

Printed bathing suits can be pretty and feminine, and the print is a good disguise of body imperfection because it draws the eye away from the pure outline. Pucci prints are pretty, polka dots are cute and perky, flowers can be sweet and feminine, especially if the suit is particularly low-cut or high-cut as the case may be. Stripes are demanding, no matter which way they run.

Should you wear a one-piece or two? A bikini is fine on a private boat, by the beach, and on a lounge chair lying down. If your body is trim they can be the most wonderful type of bathing suit because they are light and comfortable and they dry in a minute. It doesn't matter that your tummy may be a bit less than a wash board, as long as you are reasonably tan and muscular. However, by a hotel or club pool, which can be a much more intimate experience, where everyone is watching every curve, every line, every failure, avoid anything that will cause you to be insecure. Two-piece bathing suits that do not fall in the bikini category, and are highly stylised, belong only on tall, straight, small-breasted bodies with long legs. Bikinis are better with that longer length between the bra and bottoms. And they lend themselves to so many types of cute cover-ups. Tie a pareo around your bosom or wear harem pants, shorts, cargo pants, a caftan, a long see-through skirt, a divine long T-shirt. Do not tie sarongs around the lower hips unless you are slim because it will emphasise the wrong area. We could say something sensible here about burning, but we are sure you know what to do: plenty of factor 50 renewed after swimming and stay under an umbrella. The sun rays will find you anywhere.

Mature bodies have some requirements that younger shapes do not

And yet, we may be able to wear the same suits our daughters wear if we follow a few sensible rules. Look at the rear view. Try to buy a suit that cuts across your bottom in an attractive way. It will be revealed no matter what, but less is again, more. Look at the bosom area. Do you want to show your breasts in an attractive way? This requires a measure of uplift. So make sure you buy a suit that neither creates two solid grapefruits above the bathing suit line or flattens you like a gigantic double pancake below the neckline. The bandeau is a particular culprit here, widening and flattening everyone. Heart shapes are flattering and give an indication of cleavage, and straight across cuts with wide-set straps look youthful and chic.

Today's bathing suits are made of miracle fibres, and they cling and control, which is good if you are feeling a little flabby. However, too much cling, too tight, too heavy a material and your flesh will be pushed out of the suit and you will be uncomfortable.

Chose a bathing suit that emphasises your good features, complements your hair and eyes, your pretty shoulders and chest. Try to stay away from the deepest plunging necklines as too much of the mature cleavage may be revealed. Backless bathing suits can be a nice compromise, show a bit of flesh, but you must have a good, taut back.

Leopard, Tiger, Zebra et al.

Now, everyone has their opinions about wearing animal prints, and there was a time that the leopard and its relatives were chic and sexy on the beach. On young solid, smooth, unspotted flesh we might still agree. There is something erotic about animal skin and its replicas. But not so much for us. Why? It can lead towards bad taste and obviousness. The same goes for gold, silver, platinum, and diamanté. It could be cute to have a thin line of gold, or a diamanté strap, but leave it at that. You could wear a floating see-through chiffon animal print caftan over! That is elegant. We love the, usually topless, Italian and French women who wear tons of jewellery at the pool or beach. We love it because it is so outrageous, but we won't go there. You have to be born to that look, and for some reason Continental women can carry it off. However, when a large pink-breasted woman tries the same tricks at the pool, we feel embarrassment for her. Her skin is wrong, her face and her saucer-blue eyes are wrong, and her goosepimples are definitely wrong. So, just observe the look from afar and don't even think about it.

Along with your bathing suit, you will need a good-looking fabric or straw bag, some new flat clogs or slides (no high heels please, they look trashy), and a big simple straw hat in a flattering shape. Buy one that has some quality and shape and forget about that thing you got in Barbados for three dollars. It's only good for one visit. Leave it behind if you are further tempted to wear it.

If you like to wear jewellery, diamond ear studs or thin big gold hoops are good. Try a little ethnic bead necklace or a woven bracelet. No serious jewellery if you intend to swim. Many thefts are the result of gulls and their tendency to pick up shiny objects and drop them in the sea! Large tattoos are a personal choice, and we will leave it at that!

Take an extra bathing suit with you in your large straw bag, together with a good book, reading sunglasses, a scarf, suntan lotion, notepad, pen, and light eau de cologne. Then you won't have to run to your room to change or sit in a saggy wet suit till it dries out. No one wears rubber swim caps anymore, but with the price of hair colour I am sure they will eventually make a comeback. However, don't forget your hair band. If your hair is long, then tie it up in a knot when you swim. It looks neater and more attractive than your hair floating in the pool and is more socially sensitive.

No Nos.

Do keep your mobile switched off and relax. No one is interested in your domestic or work dramas by the pool. That can be so annoying.

Exercise Gear

Many disagree on this. You should pay attention to your exercise gear for several reasons: temperature and comfort. And not least: appearance. You need not have the most recent versions, but they must be spotless and look good for purpose. Going to the gym is a personal thing. You are there to keep your shape and health. Nothing wrong with looking good at the same time.

Now this presupposes that all of us need and want to exercise our bodies so as to keep our connective tissue connected, lift weights to protect our bones, and give ourselves the energy that only exercise can provide. We can play sports like tennis and golf, for which there is a broad range of choice depending on individual taste. I am afraid that if you play golf there isn't a lot you can do to make yourself look young, sexy, and feminine. It's a question of common practice and the rules that apply are comfort, suitability, and colour. Women look better when their clothes fit properly, but in golf the looseness and comfort of the attire are important to the swing. As you are out on an extended walk, you must be sure you have layers to accommodate that sudden gust of cold wind, the sun covered by a cloud, or even rain. Everything can fit in your golf bag. A divided skirt could look retro and cute with a fitted short-sleeved knitted shirt in a contrasting or matching colour, with a V-necked cotton cardigan. Keep socks short to show your ankles. Trousers should fit well across the hips and buttocks with pleats in the front or a low rise to allow movement. I like the look of a navy-blue polo shirt, greige cotton trousers with no belt, and a cable knit cotton long-sleeved sweater in a pale grey or cream. Dark clothes on the golf course, unless you are channelling the famous South African golfer, Gary Player, look a bit out of place. Shorts are for high summer, but should be above the knee, flared slightly, cut well, not too tight in the waist and in pretty bright colours. I keep mentioning light and bright. You are out on a green or beige landscape, so you need to be seen to avoid accidents. I hate a super-masculine look, like a little male clone. You can always add some pretty detail that keep you chic and appropriate. Pretty earrings, a sporty necklace, a pretty watch, and a fun hat. I like my floppy Borsalino straw hat with the tobacco-brown ribbon band.

Tennis

Tennis has its own rules, and I simply might point out that varicose veins are unattractive, so try putting on St Tropez at the start of the season if you plan to be in shorts or a short skirt. Tennis clothes should be cut well, emphasise your good points, legs, arms, shoulders, and be comfortable. Buy yourself some new ones every season to avoid that rumpled, I don't care about myself look, and make sure they wash well. Buy a comfortable soft sports bra. Tugging and pulling after every back hand is unappealing. Support is important for comfort and appearance.

White is best. Pastels could work, but some clubs will refuse you. Dark colours look like you are emulating poor Boris Becker. Light top and dark bottoms are kind of a campfire girl look. You might like it. I buy T-shirts and shorts separately and aim for style and utility. My favourite T-shirts are from rag & bone or James Perse. They wash well and do not shift shape as some do.

Shorts should be somewhat mid-thigh, slightly flared, made of natural materials, cotton or linen. They should sit slightly off the waist for comfort and looks and be well cut. Wear a string of pearls or a shell necklace. The boyish man-tailored look, as long as it isn't too masculine, has charm. As you get older, a little feminine touch goes a long way. Good fit and clean lines will make your figure look better. My pet peeve in tennis wear are artificial fabrics that look like food wrapping, ugly harsh colours in stripes and slashes, bunched up shorts that have no relationship to the proportions of a woman's body, and trendy but trashy, 'out of date in a minute' modern looks. I hate tennis dresses with no pockets so that you have to stuff the tennis balls up your underpants. Not a good look past fourteen. We need classic lines, with a bit of wit. No logos for us if it can be avoided, especially if blazoned across the chest or back, unless of course you are being paid to advertise! Have a pretty-coloured cashmere or cotton knit sweater handy to throw over your shoulders, tie around your waist, or put on when the sun ducks down. Forget the man-tailored navy blazer but do consider a cute cotton bomber jacket to wear over your shorts. Take a canvas satchel and carry sun screen, SPF 30–50, a small towel, a bottle of Evian or rosewater spray to freshen up after, and a writing pad. I always think of things that I need to do while waiting for my husband to serve!! Of course, to be noted down after the game, not during.

Skiing

For those of you who love this sport, and for me it's a kind of sadomasochism, nothing designed better to either ruin your skin, break your bones, or wrench your back, there are sports departments everywhere to meet your needs. The same rules apply to ski clothes as any other. Try to minimise your bad features and maximise the good. Padded clothes increase your size. But keep in mind, few people look good in them, apart from models. Sleeker, darker miracle materials suit most shapes. Remember to get a really fabulous pair of dark glasses. You will need them. They reek of glamour, but try not to fall on your face wearing them. By the way, though goggles are constantly pushed by sports departments, they mist up, and you cannot see a thing.

Ski hats. I love furry ones. Stay away from balaclavas unless you are planning to rob a bank to pay for your trip.

After-ski is a matter to be considered. Know your location, obviously, and discuss dress with either the travel agent, the hotel staff, or google it. Resorts vary from place to place, price to price, country to country, and its clientele.

You probably know the ones you like after all this time, so remember to buy some new and glamourous things, smart trousers, a beautiful polo-neck sweater or two in a dark rich colour. If it is a low-key low profile, hang loose kind of place, your good parka, great jeans, and some smart weather boots will be casual chic. If it is Aspen, St Moritz, Vail, Gstaad, raise the fashion ante, wear a glamourous jacket, a printed shawl, and jewellery. Go for fur-lined and trimmed parkas, and bring a long skirt, contrasting sweaters and some high heels.

Wear layers because everyone keeps their chalets very hot. In Austria and Switzerland you can do a little take on Tyrolean.

In towns like Gstaad you can find a lot of after-ski. Aspen is serious shopping. A lot of people wear fur, even these days.

Outdoor activities

Power walking, jogging, roller blading, bicycling. All these require, with few exceptions, a general type of outdoor clothes. Obviously, temperature is a factor, as well as rain, snow, sleet, wind, sun, humidity, and traffic. Bright colours with reflective strips are a service to yourself and others at twilight and beyond. If you are going on a power walk, wear either fitted exercise leggings (Lululemon have great colours) or jogging gear.

If it is cold, a layer of silky ski underwear is an idea. Layers keep the cold off but don't inhibit mobility. Good advice.

Never leave home without applying your moisturiser and eyeliner.

Carry your phone in the handy pocket manufacturers put in their leggings, in a waistband or armband. Take your credit card. You might want to stop in a shop. Never leave home without it, as they say.

Workout clothes

This section really deals with the exercise outfits that we buy in sports shops. Whether you go to a gym or exercise at home, the questions are much the same. Lycra or not. Short or long, tight or loose, cotton or miracle fibres like Dri-FIT technology, black, white or coloured, inner bra, no bra, support bra, underwear or not, modesty or let it all hang out, etc. Okay, exercise is basically something you do for yourself, and you shouldn't really worry about what you look like. Right? Wrong. When we exercise, whether Pilates, yoga, aerobics, running, conditioning, training for a marathon, or just getting ready for skiing or a favourite cocktail dress, we are still ourselves. We still want to look good, if only to that person in the mirror scrutinising us. The floppy old track pants and a worn singlet are simply not good enough to reinforce a positive ego. We need comfort, style, support, temperature control, breathability of fabric (especially if you tend to perspire excessively), and sex appeal. You can always find exercise clothes in department stores and sports shops, but my favourite shopping haunts are in hotel spas! Yes. First, they always have a good supply of fashionable things that are relatively inexpensive and if attached to a spa they may be made of natural fibres. Small brands made of cotton and Lycra are usually very inexpensive, last through 100 washings, and are young and cute. Look for yoga pants and tops with built-in bras. They are good for everything but have a slightly looser fit than your average workout leggings. Nike are a good brand, wash well, and dry quickly while perspiring, but they are kind of space-agey looking. I like something a bit more feminine and personal. After all, you may be walking to your gym! You never know who you might run into. Remember, no matter how lazy you are, do comb your hair, put it up and out of the way, and do wear a bit of lipstick and mascara. It's amazing how much better we feel and perform when we put a bit of effort into our appearance, even in the gym.

Personally, I like everything sleeveless, because I feel less constricted, but if you don't like your upper arms, go for the cap sleeve. Do not wear anything long-sleeved unless you are running outdoors in sub arctic temperatures. Then of course the classic black or navy tracksuit with woolly hat and long scarf is de rigueur. That and a pair of little stud earrings and a sports watch will take you into Starbucks attractively after. I love Lycra as it smooths out the bumps, but it should be combined with a comfortable fibre.

The bicycling short is for just that – Tour de France athletes. They show a woman's body in the most unattractive ways. I needn't spell this out and it should only be worn in desperation in the privacy of your own home.

I hate very loose knitted shorts with loose legs. Unless you like flashing, this is a very immodest and silly look destined to embarrass.

Forget nylon 'shell suits'. If you still have one, either put it in a load for Oxfam, they are still using them in out of the way corners of the world, or send them to the shredder.

If you enjoy wearing a tracksuit, buy a medium grey workout pant and hooded top in heavy cotton with a loose feel and prance out with your smart handbag and trainers. Or, if you crave warmth, nothing beats cashmere trackpants and a matching sweater. They sell them at N.Peal. Super-light, good colours, and sporty. Forget towelling unless you are fresh out of the shower. If your workout space is chilly, try dark-coloured silk long underwear. I know it sounds crazy, but they are wonderful for working out and keep your blood temperature up!!

One note on the dressing-down phenomena. Dressing-down is a kind of democratic statement. It says, as jeans once did, we are all the same, I am not pulling rank on you with my haute couture. I am savvy, I am hip, I am street cred, and I am with it. We are all prone to these trends. But like everything else that says uniformity, we rebel against the rebellion. My daughters wore school uniforms and either hiked them up or pulled them down, or shredded them, or added some strange detail so that they could seem unique. Most of us have these same urges, no matter how old we grow. On the one hand we want to be low on the horizon line, in sync with the rest of humanity, but at the same time we shout in agony at being thoroughly anonymous, so we seek out the most expensive forms of the same things that everyone is wearing. It's a conundrum. My advice is, in the realm of sports clothes, buy good but not extravagant quality. Make sure it is well kept. Wear new not terribly expensive exercise outfits, track bottoms in attractive colours with matching T-shirts and tops, and you will look elegant and correct. Carry a good sporty handbag and buy a new pair of trainers. Your real money should be invested in real clothes. Just as a thought, don't spend all your time in comfortable exercise regalia. It's a great way to gain weight and not notice. It's those elasticised waists that fool you.

Resort clothes

Why should these be any different from your summer wardrobe? Well, the climate is different, you are out of a city, in bright sun, and what looks good in summer in the city, does not look good in the Maldives, etc. White, toffee, saffron, chartreuse, beige, instead of navy and black. This is a time to indulge yourself in a fun print, maybe a charming silk or cotton skirt in a bold print or stripe with a loose linen blouse or a T-shirt, worn with flattish (a nice thick sole adds height and glamour) sandals. Above all you want to be cool, so loose, well-cut linen is a great choice, anything cotton pique, skimming the body, long wrap-around gauzy skirts with a snug T-shirt top and sandals with ties. I love the look of a sleeveless sweater over a printed chiffon skirt or loose silk trousers, with a little matching cardigan tied loosely over the shoulders. That and strappy mid-heeled mules will take you to any dressy restaurant. Take your pashminas for the cool night air, even in Mexico you might need a little cover for your shoulders after sundown.

Sunglasses: Age Defiance At The Tip Of Your Nose

Sunglasses are the mature woman's best friend. They disguise wrinkles around the eyes, reduce squinting, and protect against harmful UV rays. They give instant glamour, and some useful anonymity. If you are a person who craves privacy, then you already know about sunglasses. Think Ines de la Fressange in Chanel. Think Audrey Hepburn in Givenchy. Catherine Deneuve in YSL. Diane Keaton in Ralph Lauren. All the top designers sell sunglasses because like handbags and shoes they are good money-spinners. New models arrive in the shops with regularity and just like the young, you can plug into the latest fashion statement through sunglasses. You can have some fun with this but be careful. Pastel-tinted glasses in pink, yellow, and azure blue can give a dehydrated look. Avoid metallic frames (can injure sensitive skin on the nose), mirrored lenses, large logos on the sides, anything overly bejewelled, anything dripping in gold plate, thick, rigid black plastic, and upswept Dame Edna varieties. These are definitely not ironic on you. You need the classics: these can be circular, square, or rectangular, tortoiseshell, neutrals, greys, ambers, and dark red. If you are feeling sporty, try good old Ray-Bans, a bit retro but great for certain moods, when you feel like you are in a Steve McQueen movie. Sunglasses are essential for power walkers. They protect your eyes from dust and grit. Light frames are best for comfort, and avoid glasses that leave marks on your cheeks.

Try on lots of styles to accommodate your mood swings as well as outfits. This can be frustrating in department stores, where they have the tags hanging down. See if you can get a salesperson to remove them. If not, try a smart optician instead. In London we all swear by Cutler and Gross; in the USA Robert Marc, made by hand in Japan, super-light, super-chic.

Wear something light and pretty with summer clothes, creamy-coloured frames with dark green lenses, something darker and tougher-looking with jeans. Try something crazy now and then, huge black glasses à la Anna Wintour at night! Sunglasses are a must but avoid taking your best to the beach as sand is not kind to lenses. If you like the look of sunglasses all the time, try light-sensitive lenses, especially if they are prescription.

Some of you may have dozens of pairs of old sunglasses in drawers. These can be fun to pull out now and again but forget about resurrecting the feeling of what once was. Stick to new ones. They are better engineered these days and have a fresh feel. As a fashion statement, sunglasses are like perfume. They are attitude, ambiance, and define you as you strut down the pavement. They imply power, drama, and mystery.

Scarves And How They Work

Walking down the streets of Paris we marvel at the many twists and turns of the Parisian woman's scarves, which are made of silk, chiffon, wool, challis, leather, fur, and cashmere. They appear tied on the neck, hanging on one shoulder, draped across the shoulders and back, around the waist, looped onto her handbag, folded in half and looped through one end, fluttering from the wrist, even draped across the hips. A Frenchwoman's use of her scarf is ingenious and has loads of pizazz.

In addition to utility, the scarf is a semiotic of style. Queen Elizabeth used hers as an emblem of sportiness and her love of riding, also as a protection against the constant English drizzle. The Middle Eastern woman uses her scarves as an indicator of culture.

Utility first

Scarves come in many shapes and sizes, from the smallest handkerchief to the grandest double-sized pashmina or stole. (A favourite I bought years ago is a huge pale pink cashmere with black lace inserts from Nina Ricci, to be worn as a work of art.)

- A scarf keeps your neck and shoulders warm.
- A scarf keeps your head protected.
- A scarf threads its way through the loops of your jeans.
- A scarf protects the necklines of sweaters, coats, furs, jackets from body oil and getting soiled. It protects your newly coiffed hair. The scarf is a finishing formality of dress much like a man's tie and can be used in the same way to add a bit of colour in an otherwise conservative scheme.
- A scarf can be a substitute for jewellery.
- The scarf can emit a number of messages depending on the designer. The silk twill scarf is an expression of personality and style, status and taste, so…

Let us start with the basic Hermès scarf, that high-style arbiter of neck and head fashion. Hermès scarves are unique and you cannot have enough of them. You might think looking in your drawer, where they lie like so many jewels, how did I manage to collect so many? First and foremost the Hermès scarf is an indicator of taste and status. It comforts us with its soft luxury, its clever designs, and sophisticated colours. They are seasonal, in the sense of the four. They are seasonal in the sense of the new. They are witty, they are classic, they are geographical, literate, and they coordinate in a clever way with anything you might wear. Above all, the heavy silk prints virtually scream out class. They can be folded in a triangle, folded longitudinally, folded as a blouse, a hat, a belt, a bustier. They can be dropped inside a summer basket and used as a lining, tied around your belongings for safety. They can function as a four in hand tie or a turban. They can act as a sarong around your hips over a bathing suit, they can be used as a sling. In other words, this small and rather uncomplicated piece of fabric can express taste even if you have a broken arm, in ways that other scarves cannot because of the strength of association. After all, what is a Hermès scarf but the brilliantly designed advertising placard for a company that still makes the finest handmade, most desirable leather goods in the world. When you wear a Hermès scarf you are saying that I know what is good, what is chic, what is worth having, buying, stealing, borrowing, or inheriting.

You would never throw away a Hermès scarf no more than a Hermès bag. There is a mystique to this marque in a world of ephemera, a world of false luxury. This is the real thing and it makes everything else you wear look good.

─ ─ ─ ─ ─ ─ ─

The chiffon scarf need not have a brand name on it. Chiffon is about romance, lyricism, self-expression. It has no name, it has no price, it is simply about colour, imagination, and texture. It ties like a bow. It drifts like mist around your neck. It drapes over your bare shoulders, conceals and reveals. It looks chic bundled and tied around your neck on a suit. It covers and teases over an evening gown. It flirts and deceives over a bathing suit.

The chiffon scarf disguises any flaws in the neck, draws attention to the eyes, functions like make-up, bringing light to the face.

The chiffon scarf can be funky and shredded-looking, wispy, modern, patterned or plain.

Always tie it loosely. Don't wear it like a bandage. Keep it flowing.

Cashmere, wool, silk and wool, long or triangular scarves fall under the current appellation pashmina. Now strictly speaking, all this pashmina palaver began when the customs officials and animal rights campaigners recognised that very rich women were buying the shahtoosh from India and Nepal in great enough numbers that the tender-hearted wild antelopes that produced this fine-grade fleece were being killed to make scarves. Originally, even the hardest of fashionista hearts had bought in to the fable that the animals frolicked through bushy glades and left this softest of hairs on the bushes. Hence local farmers and peasants reaped this heavenly harvest and wove them in picturesque huts into lighter than air natural-coloured scarves to add warmth and comfort to their bodies. Like everything in our world of myth and want-to-believe romance, the reality seems to have been quite different and these charming little wild animals, living on mountaintops, were being slaughtered for their precious coats and then processed into expensive garments for wealthy buyers. Somewhere in the middle of all this lies the truth, which is that the shahtoosh, made into the finest and lightest of scarves, able to be threaded through a wedding ring, became politically incorrect. Its price was high, so it didn't affect most people anyway. In its place, or alongside, however you look at it, was born the idea of the pashmina, or stole as it was called in the old days, which is made from the wool of the Cashmere goat. This item, available now in every grade, size, and quality, in every colour, embroidered, embellished, set with stones, fringed with leather or beads, lined in fur, is now as common as running water.

Fashion writers deride its ubiquity, dismiss it as a chic statement of any kind and still it persists in every shop under every label. Why? Because it is warm. Because the colours flatter and because it adds a feminine softness to anyone who wears one. But quality, as ever, is vital. The softer and more luxurious the cloth, the more vibrant and flattering the colour. Cashmere comes in infinite grades, and you only have to run your hand over it to know that the coarser the feel, the less it is worth. Try not to buy 'pashminas' on the cheap. They wrinkle, bunch up, do not hang well, and pill. Not a formula for chic. The best ones are at Loro Piana. Hermès makes a cashmere scarf that is blended with silk. This is the all-purpose go-to and makes a statement whatever you wear it with. They never go out of style. Etro do cashmere scarves, light as a feather and blazing with colour. Again, the more neutral your wardrobe, the more monotone the colours, the more you need scarves!

Handbags

Your handbag is an expression of yourself. Never carry an inappropriate handbag, an old loose-looking scuffed appendage that screams out 'I don't care.' The handbag says many things. Quality, charm, utility, aggression, trend, money, rebellion. One or more of these statements may be yours, at any given time, but as in all things, your handbag should match the style statement you want to make, at that moment.

Now, if you can afford one, or even if you cannot, it seems that that very retro item, the Hermès Kelly or Birkin, is still the bag of the moment, even if you have to wait three years for delivery! Martha Stewart, Wall Street insider trader indictee, made the foolish fashion faux pas of showing up in court with her Birkin. Some lively editor spotted it and pilloried her up and down the press for arrogance. Well, it was good taste, style wise, but poor judgement socially. Of course, she was probably saying I am rich, I am proud, I am innocent, and I am who I am. Wrong! She should have appeared in a conservative well-cut pin-striped skirt suit, sheer black tights, sensible mid-heeled shoes, one strand of pearls, a plain black old-time Republican well-cut cloth coat, and a small black clutch, unmarked by any logo, with a pen, a pad, reading glasses, and a large handkerchief within for a tasteful tear. The Birkin did send an arrogant

message, maybe only intended subliminally. This is ultimately between her, her lawyer, and psychotherapist.

There is a lot of choice out there but there are good rules for buying and wearing a handbag.

First rule, always buy the best quality you can afford.

You need bags, obviously, for day and evening.

You need at least one day bag in black and one in tan. This is a no-brainer. But size, now that is a style puzzle.

Should a small woman wear a big handbag? Yes, when it is beautiful, stylish, and fun. The bigger the handbag in a great colour like red or purple, the better the look. Avoid, however, the carryall unless you are going to the gym. Remember your neck and shoulders when you pack it full of unnecessary items. Limit the weight.

Should a big woman wear a small handbag? Yes. When it is beautifully made or woven intricately. When it is slightly retro and hangs off your beautifully gloved wrist. A clutch is great tucked under your arm. Believe me, we all carry far too much, and this will limit you in a good way. Take one credit card, keys, lipstick and you're done.

— — — — — — —

The big shoulder strap issue. Now some physiotherapists say you should never wear shoulder straps on bags. They weigh you down, pull at your neck and shoulder areas and cause damage. I prefer to wear one, but often across the chest, basically for security reasons. I have my bag in full sight of me, not a mugger. The comfort factor is enormous. You are balanced and are hands free. Your posture will improve. There is nothing more chic than a stunning shoulder bag. It swings and says YOUTH.

Good rule to follow most of time, avoid logos. This means metal tags, buckles, hooks, and initial-printed canvas. Exceptions can be made if you have some vintage Chanel double CCs. But now logos are for teenagers. They can buy the copies, which are indistinguishable from the expensive real, so do yourself a favour and look for the subdued version when you buy.

Good places to look are Tod's. Despite their reputation as a moccasin and sandal emporium they make medium-plus-priced very smart bags. Bottega Veneta is stunning. Their prices vary, from the impossible dream to the possible, sizes for everyone, and now good new colours. They specialise in beautifully hand-woven leather items which wear well and are both calm and seductive-looking. They are light in weight, comfortable to carry and are very NOW as well as classic.

Evening bags can be made of anything from straw, velvet, suede, and metal to animal skin. I use the ones I inherited from my mother. Full of personality. An evening bag can hang off your wrist in a flirtatious way or be clutched under your arm. One warning: these days, leave your evening bag on your lap. Do not leave it on a table or on the floor. There are bag gangs everywhere we go.

Pickett London does great copies and originals. Furla is good value in the middle range. Their look is smart with lots of matching accessories. Longchamps are beautifully made and have loads of choice. French chic, leather, nylon, canvas, all sizes, all shapes, all colours. They are a Frenchwoman's must for anonymous, logo-less elegance. Mulberry is charming, sporty, and has panache.

— — — — — — —

ATTENTION: every clothing manufacturer today seems to make handbags. It's a money maker because fewer people are buying the clothes. This is how they make a profit. Some are good, some are bad, and some are ugly. Check the quality.

Loro Piana make very pricey sports clothes, the best. They also make very pricey handbags. They are canvas and high-quality leather. They double as small valises and are hand finished. They are less expensive than Hermès, more expensive than they should be, but very handsome. There is a limited supply. Tip: there is a great LP shop in Milan airport, where you can get them in the Duty Free. Very often they have things you will never see in the shops in town.

Hidden treasures

Visit Delvaux, the until recently secret resource for those who know. The Belgian version of Hermès without the hype. They have been making elite bags for decades and the wonderful thing is you can find a fabulous stylish bag for evening and day. A PR woman friend of mine has six and swears by them. No waiting list. Just drool. I love their cross-body bag that is stunning and SECURE.

Laboratorio in Capri. Designed and fabricated locally, the bags are woven masterpieces in many colours. They are the ultimate in Caprese chic. The small size is great for evening and day. The large size accommodates all your gear, wallets, keys, a scarf, a phone, the works, and again it does not shriek BRAND.

Lulu Guinness. Now, Lulu is a smart gal, and she has the kind of quirky style that could suit your granddaughter, your granny, or you. Witty, useful, beautifully made, individual, unique, and fun. They are also big enough to be utilitarian.

Prada bags are beautifully made, understated, colourful, and stunning.

Tanner Krolle bags are made of a uniquely beautiful leather with delicate detailing and are both sporty and elegant. They specialise in luggage, but their bags are smart and useful.

The Judith Leiber! At one time the most ballyhooed jewelled evening bags in the world. Fruits, animals, vegetables. If you should see one in a vintage shop, grab it! They make a big amusing statement, which will attract admiration and comment. If you have one already, wear it with a tailored dress or gown. Just don't drop it as the beads will shatter.

— — — — — — —

Talking about sustainable, handbags can be works of art, craft, and imagination. Gather them and enjoy their use. Old crocodile can be found in the antique markets, as well as embroidered bags. They can be beaded, tasselled, encrusted with paste jewels, ivory or imitation amber-handled, satin, silk, crushed velvet, metallic, gilded. Make sure they are clean within and without, and reconditioned. They won't be cheap, but they will have style and character. If you are not good in antique markets and really don't trust yourself, try Butler and Wilson on the Fulham Road in London. Etro makes fantastic bohemian elegance, including bags. Venture in and you might be surprised. I love original amusing bags. They save a lot of thinking, and you can make a bold impression with a very simple black or white pair of trousers and a shirt. Remember, style is refusal. One great accessory is enough!!

— — — — — — —

Care. Now, you may have many of the above already. You may be a tidy type who has stored all her great handbags in covers for years. Lucky you.

If not, start now. Every time you buy a good handbag, treat it like a jewel. It will serve you well. Put it away, then take out some other year. If it was a good luxurious design it lasts and has a cache that says, I always went for quality.

On the weather front, storm warning! In the rain carry a nylon handbag. Leather marks. Prada bullet-proof, heavy-gauge nylon utility bags are indestructible.

— — — — — — —

Discard time. When you have trashed a handbag, dirty, dishevelled, pock marked, and it is now an eyesore, either give it to charity, or throw it out. Actually, Cancer Research shops usually take anything. If you continue to wear it, you are saying, tired, worn-out, don't care, ancient and over.

— — — — — — —

Let's be modern. People are looking at eBay for Hermès handbags and other good brands. Be warned, they can be more expensive than in the shop, but there is probably a good reason for that. Why? Because you cannot get them in the shops! Some sellers like The RealReal are cornering the so called 'previously loved' market. Don't know how they do it, but good surfing. Do your research before you commit yourself to a bag. There are commentaries available to read on the integrity and honesty of the seller and their service. Prompt, reliable and so forth.

Sales. An opportunity or a trap?

I have heard many women say that they hate sales. They feel they are ensnared into buying things they didn't want in the first place, were trapped into buying on the second round, and discover once they are home with it that they will never use it. Having a good working knowledge of your clothes cupboard helps prevent this. But there are things that are always useful from sales. This season's shoes to replace your damaged favourites if you can find them. Great for accessories or that incredibly expensive item that by some miracle is available in your size because it is purple. You have to like purple or resist! It's a great time to buy basics, black trousers, suits, coats especially, raincoats, jackets. Try not to buy this year's trendiest thing, like the long pooled trousers with the low crotch or the oversized jacket with shoulders like helicopter landing pads.

Do not buy anything with a very political message across the chest. This season's message is next season's embarrassment. With the economy as tricky and inflation what it is, be on the lookout for the mid-season sales, when a small shop needs to offload their current stock to make room for the new! Another reason to make friends with the sales staff. They will call or write and beg you to come in to take advantage!

Belts And Other Mid-body Experiences

Try to remember that for grown-up women belts are not a functional thing to hold up your clothes. They are for adornment and fun. They spice up and define your wardrobe in ways that are flexible and new, providing shape and definition. They add attitude because they exploit the trend of the moment in an abstract way without demanding that you do the whole look. They express the idea that you are in touch with the trends and that you are smart enough to know how to put your own look together. The belt transcends age and condition. Anyone can wear a belt if they know how to accommodate their body shape. Belts have sex appeal as they emphasise the waist, the hips, the bosom, just by being where they are mid body! Belts on the hipline elongate the upper body (if you are short waisted) as well as drawing attention away from hips and derriere. As we normally age our midsections get broader and our legs and hips can get slimmer and so between waist and lower hips is a good place for a belt.

Belts stay in style because they are a complete fashion statement in themselves. They can be stored for years and trundled out to say something completely different from when you first wore them. Save all belts except mistakes. (If you hate it on sight, toss it or give it away.) Old crocodile belts are always useful, especially ones with embellishment. But make sure you know their source or you will run afoul of the Animal Rights people! Belts play with textures. Patent leather with something soft like grey flannel. Furry animal prints with something silky. Chains and grommets on something predictable and conservative. Mix it up.

The rules of belts

Forget cinched at the waist, hourglass-shaping body belts, corset belts with laces, elastic five-inch belts with 1950s connotations. Young people do hourglass better.

Avoid too much shiny gold metal and excessively glitzy chains. I have a collection of 1980s Chanel belts, but I look like I have raided Fort Knox when I pull them out. Better to sell them — or frame them. Gold plate can wear off and starts to look tacky. Pewter is okay, silver is great, blackened metal is chic. Ralph Lauren's Western belts from the 1980s are still chic now. Wear them with jeans, with Western-looking white cotton or jeans skirts, T-shirts with a leather jacket. Timeless.

Avoid all designer logos. They are obvious, boring, and dated. One year's logo is the next year's joke. But I do still love the belt I bought once in Italy that says MEXICO. I still don't understand that!

There are many women attached to their basic Hermès reversible belt. Everyone seems to have one. You see them everywhere, real and fake. They look good with jeans, skirts, and on wrap-around dresses. However, does this very nice belt still express what you want to say about yourself? If not, put in a drawer and give it a rest for the time being. Just because you continue to own it doesn't mean you are wedded to wearing it.

But if you love a certain designer and you don't want to spend money on the whole look, forget the logo rule for the moment, and buy the belt.

Wear that logo for the season and then bury it in the back garden for a decade. It will come back, they all do.

Belts are transformative. They are a jewel

Belts make black, grey, beige, and navy look interesting. The art of belt dressing is very often the juxtaposition of the classic with the somewhat incongruous, witty, daring, high fashion, or simply idiosyncratic. Make your own belt if you are creative. Old medallions or brooches attached to a leather string, or hung from a scarf? Deliciously feminine, funky and fun. We can all look for things that express our individuality.

Remember, if you choose to feature a great belt that is the one thing you concentrate on. Dispense with every other adornment (you can wear your wedding rings, watch, and simple earrings) or you will look like a Christmas tree.

Practise combinations in front of a mirror. It is all right to wear that favourite Chanel leather and chain belt with your jeans, black leather skirt, or trouser suit. But please do not do the whole Chanel nine yards: suit, blouse, chain belt, Chanel bag, logo shoes, etc., unless you have been invited to a Chanel defile, in which case disregard the above and wear it all at the same time.

Where do you find these belts that are highly individual and not blazoned with advertising? Second-hand shops. Antique clothing emporiums. Ethnic shops. Etro always has the best embellished leather and velvet belts. For day wear, use scarves as belts. Hermès has a course in folding scarves. Find out their next teaching session and try to get an invitation. Tie a scarf around your waist and fasten with a big fake brooch. Makes an amusing change. In the evening hang some pearls at your waist with a plain black silk blouse from Nili Lotan and some Chloe black trousers, pearl earrings, and insouciance! You will have the most sophisticated look around.

Belts are up!

Black always works for everyone, as long as the width is right. If you are short waisted, go for the thinner variety. If you are long waisted you can benefit from wider styles. Black belts in crocodile, ostrich, kidskin, and lizard have loads of class.

White belts are tricky, unless you are going to a garden party in a flowered dress at the height of summer, with white thick-soled sandals from French brand Clergerie and a white cotton hat (Egg on Kinnerton Street, London) that folds up to lighten up your face, or a Borsalino in pale straw with a white band. Otherwise, if you are wearing pale summer colours, tan, orange, pistachio green look better. If you are buying a shirt dress at Valentina Kova, match your belt to your shoes, but carry a different-coloured bag to avoid looking matchy-matchy. Many dresses come with self belts and that look can be improved by adding a belt that has some pizzazz. Do not be afraid.

Our Fascination With Shoes

Shoes have an importance in our world that cannot be emphasised enough. Talk about foot fetishes. And every woman has one. Open up her cupboard and you will see a psychologically driven assortment of expressions of her personality and will. They represent hours of torturous search, or complete hit and runs.

Shoes can represent devotion to one ideal configuration of the foot, or they can be a kind of promiscuity that satisfies only for one brief ecstatic moment. They are an expression of our many selves in a way that clothes can never be. Form can follow function or function can follow form, but the shoe makes a statement in itself as to how we feel about ourselves and where our vulnerabilities are.

Pass a shoe shop, stare in the window, and you will know the feeling of welling desire! It could be a tantalising high heel in peach python with a bow in the back. Not much use for anything but being lifted into a taxi and making an appearance in a restaurant. I myself have been sorely tempted by red shoes, wear them once and retire them to a prominent shelf in my cupboard, to wear when the mood hits me again.

Going hiking? You must have those black Hogans, laceless, with silver soles. Oh, yes? They murmur seductively, 'I am your younger self, I am that younger girl who runs down the street with streaming flag-like hair. I can still do that!' Or they might speak with an authoritative tone, 'I am comfortable, but I am not an old fuddy-duddy, I am in the moment.' I think this speaks of women of all ages racing around (or hobbling as the case may be) in running shoes! Shoes say all these things. They can be a long-term investment to spice up your boring suits (like the fabulous gladiator styles made by Valentino) or they are a short-term fix to give yourself a boost in an otherwise challenging day. They are life-enhancing at the very least. Where are we, after all, without our feet, our transportation, our 'places to go, and people to see', way of life!

Thank goodness the fashion industry thrives on our need for shoes. Designers who fail to produce anything of value for us are still making money from accessories and have found an outlet for their deep need to innovate. And we can wear them all.

The most important thing is to find the right shape (known as the last) and a heel height that suits you. Low heels, high heels, no heels, they all have a utilitarian and transcendent contribution to make.

Low heels

Low heels are for the very tall, the very active, the very sporty, the youthful, no-nonsense you. They look great as sandals or mules in summer with just the suggestion of a heel. Trainers, lace-up Oxfords, loafers, and flats can be elegant, comfortable, and relaxed, and can bring a dressy suit down to a manageable level during the day. If your foot tends to the long do be careful of those wonderful man-tailored brogues. They could make your feet look like they are wearing canal boats. Of course if you have the tiniest tootsies those same brogues have an androgynous playfulness.

Tod's are the ultimate player in this lowdown game, and how we love the games they play. Delicious old campsite shoes with the tiniest of heels. Moccasins in chartreuse and tomato.

And God created high heels (even Louis Quatorze wore them)

Manolo Blahnik, Christian Louboutin, Jimmy Choo, Prada, Chanel, Ferragamo, Gina, just to name a few. These designers provide the daintiest, most erotically charged shoes around. Just watch the women trying on the latest sexy take on footwear. Their eyes glaze as they wait expectantly, hoping against hope that this wonderful evocative item comes in their size. And then, oh joy, when the box arrives. And, oh happiness, when they fit, and, oh misery, when they don't or they do not fulfil their promise or are uncomfortable, or worse, make your feet look like shovels.

Now, we may be prejudiced but high heels are the kind of medicine that every woman needs. Admittedly they cannot take you through the fens or on a bicycling trip through the Normandy landing beaches. You may have foot and balance problems that may preclude the highest version. But a beautiful pair of toffee-coloured Manolo Blahnik pointy-toed shoes give you a kind of confidence that no amount of mere comfort can do. Just try a pair of stilettos and look at your legs. They are artfully stretched. The arch curves. You start 'walking the walk and talking the talk.' You feel cool; you feel long, you feel lean, you feel mean. The journey starts here. Self-knowledge and confidence that you won't trip and kill yourself.

The key to this look and this feeling is finding the right last and the right height. Okay you have a bunion. You might be suffering from an ingrown toenail. There is always podiatry. But assuming that your feet are still useable, you can do this. First rule: try the shoes on in the morning when your feet have not swelled up, and then return either later in the day or the next to try them on again. Our feet change like the weather and with the weather, so for the best fit, two tries usually works. Be very demanding. Don't apologise. If something hurts, at the throat of the shoe or on the point of a toe, or at heel, reject it immediately, no matter how much you love it. Take absolutely no encouraging guff from the salesperson. They are not wearing them. They might be able to advise you on the look of them, but do not buy shoes that don't suit your ideas about yourself. Now some of us hate ankle straps. If you have a long foot the ankle strap seems to add an inch or two to the length. In addition, if your legs from knee to ankle are not the longest, the straps cut the length even more. Ankle straps require tiny little chicken bone ankles to really flatter. The only exception to this is the nude pink colour that the ballet dancer wears. If you must have an ankle tie, buy your shoe in a pinky-flesh colour. Exceptions to the rule are the absolutely fantastic shoes shown at Valentino. Anyone no matter what size or shape can gain confidence and a feeling of power from their gladiator strap shoes, especially in beige or black. Yummy.

Toe shapes

Toe shapes vary from season to season, and pointy toes have been with us since medieval times. They flatter every foot if it is the right last. Round toes are amusing. They are bringing back round-toed Minnie Mouse shoes and they are young and fun. Try chartreuse!

Square toes are Cromwellian and ageing. Zebra-skin linen Manolos rock; grey and white snakeskin slingbacks give glamour to the most plain and conservative dress.

Word to the wise, crocodile shoes are gorgeous, cost a fortune, are stiff as boards no matter what the price, and rot when they hit the wet pavements. So unless you have money to burn and don't mind weeping over them after they have been soaked, don't bother buying them. Lizard and snakeskin are softer.

Your new elegant high heels will rule your life and change the way you walk, sit, and cross your legs. Like the Red Shoes, they will make you dance and dance. You will reach into your cupboard and bring them out to make your wardrobe feel like new. You will flex your ankles and show your knees and enjoy the process of living so much more.

Boots

Why do we wear and love boots? Is it the memory of the 1960s in thigh-high kinky black patent leathers? Or is it because they disguise flaws, support our legs, keep the splash marks off tights, fit neatly under trousers, with or without socks, and come in every height, heel, material, and colour? Or is it because they are young and feel racy. That fun transcends utility.

A good pair of boots, medium or high heeled, makes you feel female, walk better, walk taller, and they cast an erotic charge. Is it the whip/boots connection? Is it military? We all love a uniform. Is it the Puss in Boots thing, the ultimate Catwoman? Is that lovely soft leather up the calf a sensual turn-on?

In practical terms, we don't have to deal with the reality of the ankle and calf when we choose to wear boots. Some of us don't like our ankles and calves. They may be thicker than we would wish, skinnier than is the ideal: the ankle may curve nicely but might be a little too robust.

Lacrosse and ballet lessons may have knotted your muscles. The boot disguises as well as implies that what lies beneath is desirable though hidden from view. There is a bit of mystery to a pair of high boots.

To unify an outfit, same colour opaque tights and boots can perform a miracle of lengthening. The most interesting thing about wearing boots is that they bring a youthful casual attitude to almost anything you might choose to wear, within reason. It breaks the set piece, and the rigidity of the traditional skirt or suit.

Ankle boots

Ankle boots are ego time. If you have shapely calves, slim ankles, and are long from the knee to foot, this is a look that says 'notice me'. Our mothers wore them as rain or snow boots, but today's models are far from that kind of innocence. Even if your legs are less than perfection, you could wear a pair of black, stiletto high-heeled ankle boots with black opaque tights and give the world a lesson in strutting. There is a real feminine supercharge in this kind of footgear. With pencil skirts they are a must. Under trousers, they keep the illusion of the slim leg underneath and provide comfort, warmth, and protection. Evening versions come in suede, brocade, or satin with tiny diamanté buckles. They can give a bohemian fillip to a longish evening skirt and strict jacket.

Trainers, etc.

Trainers, sneakers, tennis shoes, high tops, designer styles, to be worn with everything? That is the question?

One cannot fail to notice the trend that has grown and grown in the last several years of wearing trainers or sneakers, lace-ups, etc., with everything. Magazine editors style them with flowery long dresses, skirts, and wide-legged trousers. They show them with soles the size of shoes boxes. I rather like that look as they make you taller! They come embellished with shiny stones; at Golden Goose they come pre-aged. The soiled look comes at a premium. They are available in every colour, size, and shape, at every shop.

Do you want this look? And if you do, what does it do for you? On some level it is again the search for the evanescence of youth, that disappearing commodity we once had. Throw on a T-shirt and a pair of sawn-off jeans, wear a pair of Keds and race out with your boyfriend to the beach, kind of thing. That feeling is behind the popularity of this style, as well as their comfort and casual appearance. But what if this footwear makes you look sloppy, old and weary, and consigns you to the borders of orthopaedic footwear? I like to wear trainers when I am in jeans. I like them with tennis shorts and golf clothes. I enjoy them in summer on a walk, and in winter to keep my feet warm and dry. They have a use... and I am agnostic about what others decide.

The Eternal Feminine

How middle-aged women can overcome their fashion frustrations and turn on their style.

Before we give any further advice, do follow this absolutely vital rule. HIT THE SHOPS AS EARLY IN THE SEASON OR PRE-SEASON AS YOU CAN. You will find the right sizes and colours. You won't run out weeping with the unfairness of it all. Also, make friends with the purveyors of clothing in your local shops, discuss your needs, and ask them to notify you when something suitable comes in. Shopping is an ordeal for many, but if you plan well, it can be less heart-breaking, especially if you need something. What could be worse. You are going to a special event, and you have NOTHING TO WEAR! And there is nothing to buy! That is when knowing thyself and having the ability to combine and think through what you have comes in handy.

Sources are a complicated matter. There are many guidebooks on shopping, advising you what shops to go to, what mean streets you drag yourself down, lurching from one supposedly hot spot after another and finding exactly nothing. There are loads of websites... too many in fact for us, as buying online is a tricky business. Talk about unsustainable! So many things are returned that there's even more air pollution as a result!

There are always new shops. You read about them in the papers: you go in there expectantly. There could be lots of choice, but Nothing for You. In order to guide our constant reader, seeker of fashion style and elegance, she has to question herself. Who am I? What do I want to be today or tomorrow for that matter, and how do I get the look?

Let us break this down into some basic types as opposed to treating middle-aged women monolithically, avoiding being fattist or thinnist, because what we think about ourselves is not always dictated by size. Though, for the larger or tinier of us, it is an extra problem to face, in addition to limited choice.

Tall ladies can want to appear feminine and girly.

Short women can have big stature.

Heavy-set women may be light on their feet and flirtatious.

Skinny little social x-rays can be beautifully dressed but a bit scary-looking.

Ça depend, say the French. Personality is everything in life.

Joy, happiness, the ability to charm others is a gift, and it is very independent of size, shape, or even money! When we dress ourselves we look to charm, to entrance. Styling ourselves in the most attractive way lifts our spirits and when we are happy within ourselves, we make others happy.

Who Are You These Days?

Still rebellious after all these years?

You refuse to conform. You always wore the latest and most outrageous of styles. Comme des Garçons was you. But now it looks a bit passé. Forget Comme, it's too outrageous, but Yohji Yamamoto and Issey Miyake are still a possibility, especially in larger sizes. Just remember to accessorise correctly when you buy something a bit avant-garde. Ask the salesperson what shoes and bag go best with the look.

There is an entire world of designers, Ann Demeulemeester, Dries Van Noten, Helmut Lang, Marni, Etro, not to mention those small French and Italian brands like Casey Casey that could satisfy your desire for uniqueness and rebellion against conformity. However, sizes could be a problem. This look is easy to find, but hard to edit. Try to avoid doing the whole top-to-toe thing. Buy one interesting piece, a shirt/jacket, a pair of trousers, a dress, and combine with something simpler and more classic, a black leather jacket, a polo-neck sweater, under a knee-length classic coat. The problem with sorting through these designers in department stores is the way they are displayed. Always on hangers, not made to work in the real world. If you can find a salesperson, ask what goes with what. There is always a 'look book' which shows the collection as the designer intended it. It may help you visualise. The smaller shops seem more adept at helping you pull the look together, and of course they want to sell!

Classically elegant like our mothers wore

Suits, cocktail dresses, tailored coats and dresses, well-cut trousers and jackets for sporty outings, dressing gowns, floating caftans (like Zsa Zsa Gabor), in other words the 1950s. No matter how good they looked then, those clothes are dated and ageing today. However, you can find the new editions of this look in our favourite top of the tree brands. Chanel, Akris, Celine, Ralph Lauren, Caroline Charles, Alberta Ferretti, Jil Sander, Valentina Kova, YSL, Louise Kennedy London. At the mid end: Hobbs, L. K. Bennett, Zadig & Voltaire, Sandro, Me & Em, Bimba y Lola. At the low end: H&M and Zara. Remember our shopping rules. Get friendly with the sales personnel. They are supposed to know their stock and how it should work for you. Ask them to set things aside till the entire look comes in. Get to the shop early in the season. Personalise and update this look with your jewellery, fun handbags, etc. Always put your own stamp on this, not what Mother would do. Loosen up. Wear boots, wedges,

platform sandals with bare legs when Mummy wouldn't. Wear a fur scarf and fur-trimmed gloves. not a fur coat. Wear fabulous fake jewellery. Do a huge Swarovski beetle brooch instead of good pearls. Wear garnets and citrines instead of diamonds. Go a little longer or shorter than you usually would do. If you have great legs, an inch above the knee is great. If you are not keen on your legs, an inch below. Legs are sexy. Because everyone wants to dress down these days, smart casual it is called, try to break up the look. If you love wearing a wonderful tailored jacket, put it with jeans or wide trousers. If you have a fabulous little black dress, mix it with ankle boots with a mid-heel and lots of bracelets up your arms. Wear a cape instead of a coat. If you wear a trouser suit, accessorise with a cross-body bag and high heels, and dinner-plate-size earrings.

Intellectuals but not bluestockings (you are not a prude)

This is tweedy, subdued, conservative, but with a fashion-forward twist because you want to be taken seriously, but you want to project femininity. Who's the best uber-minimalist: Armani (whispers intelligence and high standards), Margaret Howell, Prada (not everything she does is trendy), Rick Owens, Bottega Veneta. Try this look: Grey well-cut trousers and a pale grey polo-necked sweater, small lizard-look belt slung on the hip line, and a loose jacket by Casey Casey in camel hair with Cuban-heeled boots. Wear some amber beads round your neck. Tiny gold drop earrings and some contrasting amber and jet bracelets make an intellectual but stunning hit. Take your cues from the women curators at museums who lead talks. They usually look great, have chosen their clothes as statements of their intellectual prowess and professionalism, but still manage to look feminine and chic.

Working women who multitask

They are often part of the sandwich generation, dealing with children, husbands, and ancient parents. There is a uniform that applies to any number of occupations, e.g., law, the City, medicine, business. Basically you need utility. You need to look serious. You need a jacket. You need a tailored skirt or trousers. Even if you are in a Zoom, the top end has to look as if you are professional and in charge. White silk shirt. Black or navy fitted or knitted jacket. Scarf around your waist, and some small but meaningful earrings. Light make-up, blusher, and mascara. Ready for your close-up!

Though a highly successful banker or lawyer might wish to wear, on some occasions, a Chanel or Armani suit, the rule for working women should be very smart, but don't outdo your client. A proper suit is almost impossible to find. In London you could try Louise Kennedy, or Claudia Sebire. In the USA there are a myriad of brands, many of which are European, but you could try Michael Kors, or Carolina Herrera. Create a look out of separates if you must.

Use our rules. Smart Prince of Wales dark blue-grey jacket with an indented waist, grey flannel or gabardine skirt to the mid-calf, antique lace handkerchief in pocket for a bit of dash, navy or black silk blouse, sheer tights, smart kitten-heeled Christian Louboutin court shoes, silver and stone necklace, small silver or diamond stud earrings, and a smart steel and gold watch. If you have a Rolex or can get one, good for you!

Serious and smart.

Bohemians, by nature, not necessarily by occupation

Different from rebellious. This has been your look, long-term. You have always loved long ethnic skirts, grungy crinkled trousers, embroidered waistcoats, floppy hats, and long dangling earrings. You might still be wearing rose-tinted granny glasses and lace-up boots. Hey babe, get over it. You will look like a bag lady if you continue to do this into your afternoon of life. Do one thing, maybe two, but not everything at once. Long skirts with fitted sweaters, embroidered vest or jacket with well-cut blue jeans. Try Monsoon, Paul Smith, Kenzo, Etro, Issey Miyake, rag & bone. Try ethnic jewellery shops for Moroccan silver and beads, and batik-dyed scarves. Wear some Bakelite or faux tortoiseshell bangles or Chinese cinnabar. In London, haute bohemians can accessorise their look at Grays Antique Market, Alfies, Butler & Wilson, or Liberty. Try Portobello Market on Saturday morning. Ermanno Scervino at the top end is a combination of sex appeal, lace, leather, and good tailoring. A great bohemian look at night is a pair of black silk jersey cut trousers with a three-quarter-length, patterned coat with lace trim. That and velvet pointy boots and a big turquoise silver ring and bangle make your statement. Look for these things in shops that feature one-off pieces like those made by the Canadian designer Zonda Nellis or tie-dyed silk full-length evening coats. When in Capri visit Laboratoria or Blu. They have the best silk coats which create a relaxed but totally elegant look. I wear my white jeans with a white silk trench coat down to the ground with a T-shirt and espadrilles and loads of pearls.

Artistic types.
Same as previous. But even wilder

Okay, you paint or write all day. You want others to know this. What is your basic look apart from stained jeans and a smock? For some it is high-heeled boots, Armani jeans, the no-nonsense white T-shirt (Loro Piana), an emerald brooch, and a funky Chez Vidalenc Parisian jacket. This projects a creative spirit in a stylish, but relaxed and knowing way. (Remember to clean your fingernails with turps at the end of the day.) Wear a long flowered skirt with a snug sweater, and a very glitzy, diamanté-laden jeans jacket that looks like a corset from Dolce & Gabbana. Pinned to that is your granny's brooch. You may need a stiff drink to try this, but it says artiste, free spirit. It takes a lot of taste to put things together that are in opposition. A lace blouse over jeans is not for everyone. Diamonds at breakfast on black working gear is a stretch. But I have seen it done. Louise Kennedy, the designer, always wears a mix of diamonds, old and new. They declare her as a creative woman who has succeeded in her own world and is wearing her rewards. By the way, the greatest thrill aside from first love is to buy a serious piece of jewellery for yourself. I recommend a pair of diamond clips from Hancocks in the Burlington Arcade. They have the best of the past... and each piece is a bit of magic for any outfit.

Corporate ladies, top of the food chain wives or others

Very similar to working women, because this is real work in the real world. You must dress for success, but at the same time not overly flaunt your husband's wealth, or status. You must not be overtly sexual. It is like being a doctor. On the one hand, no one wants a doctor who looks like a poor slob. Neither do we want a doctor who looks, in his handmade crocodile shoes, as if he is making a fortune off your misfortune. So there is a delicate line to tread. This may be a time when you must subdue your instincts for attention. We are talking serious clothes, elegant clothes for evening entertaining. You want admiration, maybe a tiny bit of envy, but not too much. Now is the time for the little black dress, the beautifully cut Giorgio Armani black crepe pant suit, the Chanel jacket (real or unreal), worn with a black skirt. Think Prada, Louise Kennedy, Stewart Parvin, Bruce Oldfield, Celine. A prescription for the ultra-smart corporate conservative look is the beautifully cut plain dark black cashmere coat with a bit of fur trim over mid-calf-length beaded black silk chiffon skirt and black cashmere sweater with black suede boots. A small black crocodile or silk satin bag completes this look.

Au naturals, make-up free (?), braless, and couldn't care less

There is a stylish way to deal with this anti-style phenomena. Sports clothes. Think Katherine Hepburn, Lauren Hutton, Ralph Lauren Polo advertisements, think country. It's too late for au natural unless you seriously want to look your age.

Tinted moisturiser, Touché Éclat, Clarins moisturiser, lip gloss, just a lick, dark brown mascara, nude polish from OPI or better still a regular manicure, pale rose blusher lightly applied for those cheeks. Braless? Please. Go quickly to the bra department, and buy a good, rounded shape. Do not listen to anyone but your own good sense. Try a silk camisole from Hanro.

Sporty shops. Polo Ralph Lauren, Loro Piana, Margaret Howell, Farlows fishing shop, Barbour, Holland & Holland, Hermès (for loose-cut clothes and padded jackets, you may need to consult with your bank manager here). Cashmere tracksuits look better than towelling. Try some trainers from Stan Smith. Au natural is difficult because the older you are the more it can look like laziness not 'devil may care' insouciance. It's an awful truth but au natural is the hardest look to achieve with style. There are so many casual chic shops around featuring loose gathered trousers, T-shirts, chinos, jeans. You are the blessed as there is plenty of choice. Favourite look from Egg London is a long white skirt with T-shirt, distressed silk jacket that looks as if it has been through the washing machine 100 times and it probably has to make the look! Clergerie sandals with super-thick soles, ankle straps, and a big white fabric hat. Max Mara is for the sporty and you will find all the pale and neutral colours you might like in a variety of cuts and fabrics. I love linen for that au natural look of complete self-assurance.

Rich as Croesus without a social conscience

If you want to risk your life everyday by looking seriously rich, we have a few suggestions. A large car driven by a chauffeur is a must. May I suggest the Bentley SUV, navy blue the most tasteful. Haute Couture from anyone, anywhere, very large Graff, Moussaieff or Harry Winston diamonds, or for casual wear, equally large David Webb bracelets and earrings, Park Avenue, Houston, Palm Beach locations. Try Richters, Palm Beach, for the real thing from the days when David Webb was alive and designing gigantic animal jewels. For slumming, reserve the entire collection of Chanel well before the season and call up for delivery and a bottle of Dom. You will only need Manolos because you must never walk alone on the street. Fur coats, from J. Mendel NYC, preferably sable, and sculpted nails. Someone else can punch in your telephone numbers on your platinum mobile phone.

Rich as Croesus with a social conscience

This is more difficult. The large black Mercedes hybrid SUV driven by a homeless person you have transformed. Armani navy blue suit with Loro Piana white T-shirt, plain grey gabardine raincoat, and an earnest look. Antique Mehlman Georgian rose-cut diamonds for some shimmer not bling. From Macklowe Gallery, NYC, classic art deco rings and brooches, and handmade low sensible shoes by Lobb. Carry your oldest Birkin, with socially conscious magazines tucked in like *The Green Party Guide*, *The New York Review of Books*, and either a Márquez or Borges novel. Take off your sunglasses for direct eye contact with the masses. In order to be authoritative at charity meetings, always wear your glasses, leave your contacts home; if your eyesight is still good except for distance, bring out the half reading glasses. In the evening, a black gabardine trouser suit, impeccably cut, black crocodile or silk Roger Vivier shoes, a discreet 1937 Cartier diamond flower brooch, a small, black ribbon diamond watch, antique or modern, very spare, and a marcasite lorgnette, useful for reading opera programmes in your box, or the menu at dinner at The Links Club NYC. Nothing too trendy-looking, but always incredibly expensive.

Ladies who look like they lunch

Skirts with an expandable waistband are useful. Find a reliable tailor/designer and explain your problems. The wonderful Stewart Parvin on Motcomb Street is a magician. If you have added several pounds to your dimensions, on the retail side, there is Marina Rinaldi, Bond Street and their designs are for heroic women who are still very interested in looking chic. Eskandar, Egg, Issey Miyake, Yohji Yamamoto, Akris are very handy after a big meal.

Ladies who lunch but not often

Always well-groomed and stylish in a casual world. They have found the balance. These women don't eat excessively, watch the pounds, they exercise regularly, take vitamins by the handful, maintain vigilance. They are found in NYC, Chicago, and Paris, wearing everything. They know how to put it together. They have an instinct for fashion. They are goddesses and if you spot one, remember what she was wearing. In art class you always learn more from the person drawing or painting next to you than you do from the teacher! Style is the same. Keep looking and copy anything you like. I adore analysing my super-chic friends and parsing in my mind how they put things together.

The truth seekers

There are those of us who combine all the previous instincts about fashion but have their own things to say. They are the chosen few. One day they are goddesses, the next day they are tramps. They like to play. The look for evening can range from haute ensemble, black Chanel with extremely expensive tattered embellishments, to high bohemia, tight jeans with a Prada blouse and stringy hair. They wear navy tailored suits to business meetings, high heels or moccasins with a girl scouts' shirt and depend on accessories. They have a supply of past wardrobe solutions which they use with wit, making choices and combinations at will. They wear jeans with expensive jackets, skirts, and Manolos to show off their legs.

How do they acquire this endlessly interesting, changeable look? They are always on the lookout for something imaginative like sniffer dogs. One way to get current and re-invent is to look in antique markets. Vintage top to toe is not a choice for the mature woman because it can look tired and dowdy. However, now that women are seeking a more classic look reminiscent of the 1950s, there is a demand for the accoutrements of that period. In the antique markets you can find designer scarves, half price and nearly new; good 1950s or 1960s costume jewellery, and the highest quality vintage handbags. They are not cheap. But they are available, in good quality, and make a lot of sense if you want the look but are not comfortable with looking on eBay or waiting a year for a bag to come up in the shop. And what about social responsibility, recycling?

- - - - - - -

Note of interest. It is charming and touching to see how beautifully looked after, sometimes in their original boxes, vintage jewels of style were. Our mother's and our generation valued their precious bags, jewellery, handkerchiefs, gloves, and preserved them. These beauties represent a different attitude to lovely things. There was no irony. These were the things dreams were made of, and they were respected.

There is a quality and sentiment to these artefacts that provide a kind of truth, an authenticity and originality that cannot be found these days except at an enormous price.

If you have the time, this is a kind of aesthetic re-education. Our daughters are already learning from the past by looking at vintage. They too are fed up with what they are being offered in the shops.

Anyway, you get the picture. We are grown-ups with different personalities and needs but we are all looking for a road to style, the fun of shopping, without necessarily taking out a mortgage every time we venture out, the thrill of the chase and capture of that wonderful thing.

Conclusion

We have been writing on the subject of grown women's frustrations with the fashion industry given their financial power, their longevity, and self-maintenance. We have given lengthy advice on having fun, getting stylish, being yourself. We are being positive about the ageing process. But, in addition to voicing our disgruntlements, learning a few tricks for freshening up our existing apparel, we can do something other than complain. Ask questions in a shop. Make demands. There is a shopping re-evaluation happening as we speak. People are not spending money. We are careful with our money. Suggest ways to your local shop's manager as to how they can improve our loyalty, get us to visit regularly and spend.

On a visit to Prada the other day, looking through the racks, trying on shoes, watching the other shoppers, Kaaren noticed that there were a number of women who were smart-looking, but definitely a little longer in the tooth than the Chinese teenagers the shop usually has in abundance. They were patting handbags, trying on shoes, and leafing through fun jackets in pale sand nylon. They looked at the clothes but were buying shoes. As she was thinking about the purpose of this book, while paying her bill for a delicious pair of kitten-heeled sandy-pink slingbacks and a matching cashmere sweater to wear with an ancient leather skirt, she asked the woman at the till about the clientele. Who were they? Were there any sizes for them? Her answer was a bit cryptic. She replied that she had read that the average age in Britain was forty, so it only made sense for the Prada brand to accommodate the older and sophisticated shopper.

There was a look of commiseration but no answer.

Women, rise up. Make your voices heard. Don't just settle for a wallet. Get the whole look you are after. And, hey there, manufacturers, what about producing clothes that represent all the different body shapes? Your prices are sky high. So what is wrong with your financial model?

The industry must come to some kind of self-assessment to accommodate the adult woman. The emphasis is always on youth, but youth and youthfulness are relative. Prices are far too high. Style is missing. Old designers are grappling for meaning and not finding it. New designers are suppressed by the costs as well as a lack of understanding of the needs of women of today, including the more mature. The designers and buyers need to rethink and reprice. Mostly they need to show respect for us. We were the leaders, the doers, the thinkers for the future. The current generation inherited our guts and our hopes for all women, whatever their choices.

We demand your attention!

Made in the USA
Columbia, SC
19 January 2025

Made in the USA
Columbia, SC
19 January 2025